Sikhs, Russians & Sepoys

James P. Robertson

Sikhs, Russians & Sepoys

Recollections of Campaigning With the 31st Foot
and Military Train Cavalry in the First Sikh War,
Crimean War and Indian Mutiny

ILLUSTRATED

James P. Robertson

LEONAUR

Sikhs, Russians & Sepoys
Recollections of Campaigning With the 31st Foot and Military Train Cavalry in the First Sikh War, Crimean War and Indian Mutiny
by James P. Robertson

ILLUSTRATED

First published under the title
Personal Adventures and Anecdotes of an Old Officer

Leonaur is an imprint of Oakpast Ltd

Copyright in this form © 2020 Oakpast Ltd

ISBN: 978-1-78282-898-3 (hardcover)
ISBN: 978-1-78282-899-0 (softcover)

http://www.leonaur.com

Publisher's Notes

The views expressed in this book are not necessarily those of the publisher.

Contents

QUEEN'S COLOUR

REGIMENTAL COLOUR.

THE 31st COLOURS

DEDICATED TO THE
RIGHT HONOURABLE R. B. HALDANE, M.P.,
SECRETARY OF STATE FOR WAR,
IN GRATEFUL REMEMBRANCE OF THE LIFE-LONG FRIENDSHIP
THAT EXISTED BETWEEN THE AUTHOR AND HIS
NOBLE-HEARTED AND WORTHY FATHER
THE LATE EGBERT HALDANE OF CLOANDEN

Preface

In giving these pages to the public, I feel rather nervous, from the remark that my publisher made—'Some of your adventures are almost incredible.' I do honestly assure my readers that I only put down facts, and I think I may truly say that I have had a long life wonderfully protected by a gracious God through more hairbreadth escapes and wonderful experiences than fall to the lot of most men.

When quite a small child I was taken to bathe at Portobello, near Edinburgh, by the companion and friend to my grandmother, Mrs. Stuart of Fincastle, who spent her latter years at Portobello. As soon as my things were taken off I jumped into the sea, waded out till I was carried off my feet, and rolled under till my lungs were full of water, when all feeling of suffocation disappeared, and I felt quite comfortable looking through the water above me like rough green glass. The colour gradually deepened till it became black, and then I was insensible and drowned to all appearance—in fact, I went through the whole experience of a drowning man, but a lady in the next machine saw a little white hand above the water, and rushed in and carried me out. When I came to myself, I was lying on the floor of the bathing-machine, being well rubbed.

A few years after, I fell and damaged my skull while looking at fireworks from the top of the garden wall. I fell off the rocks at Prestonpans, and damaged my left leg so badly that I was months in bed. Then it was discovered that, from lying so long on one side, my spine was twisted, and I remember Dr. James Simpson and another doctor putting their cold fingers all down my back. I had to be cased in steel for two years, and was taken to Carron Vale, where I ran wild and did no lessons, and after this I returned to the High School in Edinburgh, where I had a bad fall at football and had a stone knocked right into my knee-cap, which kept me in bed for six weeks.

Then, when on a visit to my cousin at Callander, I took a fancy to see what was in a magpie's nest on the top of a larch-tree. I set up the stable-ladder and from that took to the branches. When just under the nest, the branch I was standing on broke short off, and down I fell to the ground, fortunately missing the ladder. I hit my head against the tree and lay quiet for some time, feeling none the worse, and just put back the ladder and said nothing about it.

The history of my face alone would fill a chapter. When quite a small boy I got the present of a toy cannon. All boys had them in those days, and fired them all day long on the queen's birthday. This custom has long since died out. On this occasion I found my cannon nearly full of paper, and to get that out I took a bit of strong wire, made it red-hot, and tried to burn the paper out, when, in consequence of being already loaded, bang! went the cannon, and the wire shot through the lobe of my right ear and stuck in the ceiling of the room. My dear mother came in and requested me not to fire any more in the house. The ear got all right again, but to this day is a different shape from the left.

When I was trying to blow up a wasp's nest, the mine of coarse blasting-powder went off in my face, and peppered it full of unexploded large grains of powder. I went to my room and with a gold pin dug out every grain, cleaning the wound with my nail-brush. It was a most painful operation, but if I had left the powder in I should have had a blue face for life, like my ancestor Graeme of Inchbrakie, who bore the sobriquet of Black Pate from an accident of the same kind.

A fall out hunting smashed the bone of my nose into little bits, and on another occasion, I fell on a rock, and my two front teeth came through the skin below the under-lip.

After the above by no means full list of accidents in my younger days, possibly my friends will be prepared for some startling personal adventures in after-life. My dear mother used to say, 'Oh, laddie, laddie, you'll come to some awful death if you don't take more care of yourself!' But here I am at the patriarchal age of eighty-four, able to take a twenty-mile run or more on my bike and without a mark or damage on my face, but please remember that I have been for many years a total abstainer, and I never went into any fight or battle on anything stronger than cold tea. The bare list of my horse and carriage smashes would fill pages, and some of them you'll get in their right places, but I must spare you for the present.

The Author.

September, 1906.

CHAPTER 1

First Voyage to Calcutta

I was born on January 26, 1822, at Carron Vale, the property of my father, the Honourable Duncan Robertson, M.D., who owned also an estate near Callander known as Roehill, or, in the Gaelic, Knock-Carrup. On the top of a little mound, standing in the north-west corner of this property, two march walls crossed at right angles, and the four proprietors could stand each on their own land and shake hands at the same time.

My grandfather, James Robertson, owned a small estate on the south bank of Loch Tay, and was a married man with a son six years of age when Prince Charlie landed in Scotland. It is a matter of history that the Robertson clan loyally joined the prince, with the disastrous result that the Campbells cleared them out of Loch Tayside, when my grandfather took refuge in Callander.

I believe he only saved his life by having married one of the Campbells of Monzie; and it is a remarkable fact that, while my paternal grandmother was a Campbell, my maternal grandmother was Louisa Graeme of Inchbrakie—the two properties were contiguous in Strathearn and thus two of my ancestors were concerned in the Perthshire history of the burning of the 'Witch of Monzie.'

It is a well-authenticated fact that Graeme of Inchbrakie exerted himself to save the woman's life, while Campbell of Monzie insisted on her being burned, and carried his point. The so-called witch, when tied to the stake, flung a precious stone at Inchbrakie, saying: 'As long as your descendants hold this stone your property will be secure, and descend from father to son.' Monzie she cursed with failure of direct line of descent. Both of these remarkable prophecies have literally come true. Not long before Inchbrakie was sold, the stone, set in a ring, was removed to Edinburgh in complete disregard of the con-

11

ditions stated in the witch's last words. Monzie has never since descended from father to son.

To return to my father: he was educated for the medical profession, and settled for many years in Jamaica, where he practised as a physician, and as a Member of Council got the title Honourable, eventually becoming owner of a very fine estate there called Friendship. I should like, while referring to him, to record a very remarkable matrimonial chain which commenced quite early in the eighteenth century by the marriage of a young man, then living in Jamaica, who started the chain. In his old age he married a second wife who was quite a young girl, a Miss Lutman. During her husband's last illness, my father, Dr. Robertson, attended him professionally; and he made the very extraordinary request to my father that he would, after a reasonable period, marry the young widow, who had no near relations living in the island. This he did, and became owner of part of Friendship; the other half he purchased from Mr. Lutman, his wife's brother; and the whole estate thus became his property.

After many years of happiness, Mrs. Robertson died, and sometime after my father returned to Scotland and married my mother, Susan Stuart of the royal Stuarts of Fincastle. She was the youngest daughter of Colonel Robert Stuart, of Fincastle, and Louisa Graeme, of Inchbrakie, his wife. To make a long story short, about twelve years after my father's death, my mother married Dr. Liddell, who was the first Principal of Queen's College, Kingston, Canada, and who afterwards, on account of my mother's health, returned to Scotland, and became the parish minister of Lochmaben in Dumfriesshire, where he lived for about thirty years, dying in 1880, and thus ending the matrimonial chain of more than 150 years, my mother having predeceased him. In her brother, Peter Stuart, ended the line of Fincastle. Many old Perthshire families have thus disappeared within my own lifetime.

When out in the Maroon War in Jamaica, my father had a narrow escape of his life. He was shaving one morning in the open air, having hung up a little glass against a tree, when one of the enemy fired a poisoned arrow at him, cutting his chin open. Knowing the deadly nature of the wound, he, with his razor, cut the piece clean out on the spot, and thereby saved his life. The mark of the wound is clearly to be seen in his portrait, painted by Sir Henry Raeburn, which hangs in my dining-room.

To return to myself: I determined to leave home after my mother's second marriage, and went off quietly to London, and got a berth as midshipman on board the *London*, one of Wigram and Green's East Indiamen—'free traders,' as they were then called, on account of the East India Company having lost their charter and privileges. Nothing very remarkable occurred during our passage to Calcutta, but one day I was ordered to go with one of the quartermasters, who had something to do in the magazine.

The magazine was a strong iron room, down in the after-hold, where all the cabin stores were kept. My orders were to sit at the scuttle and hold a lantern so that he could see. The quartermaster was sometime fussing about; he had evidently got hold of something very nice before he got to the magazine.

Presently I heard the iron door open, and I got a peremptory order to come down with the lantern, as he rather noisily informed me, with a good deal of strong language, that he could not see what he was doing.

I accordingly went, and held the lantern up outside the open door. After fumbling about for some time, he ordered me to come inside, lantern and all. In I went, and sat down on a bag of powder. Presently, after some more fumbling, I got the order, 'Take the candle out of the lamp and hold it in your hand.'

'Oh dear!' I said; 'what would the captain say if he knew this?' To which my friend replied, with a fresh edition of strong language intermixed:

'I know just as well as the captain that, if you drop that candle, we will all be in hellfire in less than five minutes.'

Need I say how I crawled out most carefully, nursing the candle till I got well outside. Of course, I dared not tell the captain, or anyone else, or my life would not have been worth living. On board no one ever peached on another.

When we were going round the Cape, blowing hard, and the wind right aft, I had just turned out of my hammock for morning watch (4 a.m.), when the ship suddenly broached to, and a tremendous sea broke right on board of us, and came thundering down the main hatchway, which was wide open. I shall never forget the comic scene which ensued. The doctor jumped out of bed, and sent his head right through the Venetian blinds with which all the cabin doors were furnished for ventilation. There he stuck, with his face a perfect picture of horror.

At the same time a young cadet rushed out of the cabin, went wildly along the deck, burst through the after-cabin doors, and rushed into the arms of three young ladies, who were on their way to Calcutta, on 'spec' as we used to call it in those days. By this time the steerage was half full of water, and the young gentleman was speedily rolled up in a blanket, head and all, and shot back into the water.

But the most comical sight of all was the captain. He was a rotund little man, and he jumped out of his cabin in his shirt to make his way on deck; but he had scarcely got outside his door, when a lady, with no particular garments on, rushed at him, seized him round the neck, screaming, 'Oh, save me! save me! save me!' To see the captain struggling to get rid of her arms was a sight worth seeing. For myself, I had such unbounded faith in the ship, that I did not feel the least alarmed, and with a good supply of buckets, and plenty of hands, we soon cleared all the water out again.

Although quite at home in any part of the rigging by night or day, I had a very trying and dangerous—I may say awfully dangerous—job one day. After getting into the 'trades,' the captain ordered the skysails to be set. Now, skysails are, as the name implies, at the very top of the masts. I was ordered up to set the mizzen-skysail, which was then on deck, and the halyard by which it was to be hauled up had to be carried up by me and passed through the head of the mast, just under the vane. Up I went, with the long rope coiled loosely and hanging on my shoulder. I had no difficulty in getting as far up as the royal yard, but just above that the rigging ended, and there was nothing but a pole well-greased and perfectly smooth.

To the top of this, about ten feet high, I had to climb with the heavy bundle of rope, and pass the end through the top of the mast and pull it through. A slip meant certain destruction, and there was nothing but the greasy pole to hold on by, and it was swinging to and fro with the motion of the ship. I was mercifully preserved, and came safe down again. It was about the most unpleasant bit of work I ever did in my life, worse than facing a man with a drawn sword or a loaded rifle.

We were nearly three months in Calcutta, discharging and taking in cargo.

On our return passage home, an outward-bound ship hailed us to say that the king was dead, and that Queen Victoria was on the throne.

It is rather remarkable that the three middies who sailed on board the *London*, myself and two others, all joined the army: Grossman into the East India Company's service, Harrison into the Royal Marines, and I joined the 31st Regiment.

14

On my return to London, Mr. William Morris, I may say, took charge of me. He was a West India merchant, and had a large and extensive connection in Jamaica, where our property Friendship was.

The slaves having been freed in the West Indies, things began to look very black, and Mr. Morris was very anxious to go out to look after his own interests. He owned a ship called the *Black River Packet*, and soon made arrangements for the voyage, taking me with him.

As is now a matter of history, our West India possessions were ruined by the haste and over zeal which, in my opinion, far outran the knowledge of the good people at home.

To begin at the beginning, the African savages who were exported to the West Indies were, to a great extent, prisoners taken in war; they were brought down to the coast, sold to Europeans, and taken comfortably across to the West Indies. I say 'comfortably' advisedly, because there was no object in treating them otherwise, for the 'fitter' their condition on arriving at their destination, the more capable they were of doing their work on the estates, and thus fetched a higher price. When our men-of-war began to scour the coasts to capture the ships containing these negroes, in order to avoid the English ships the 'traders' huddled the poor wretches together and packed them like herrings in a barrel into very fast sailing 'slavers'; even so, those who got to the West Indies were the most fortunate.

On every estate there was a hospital and a competent medical man paid a fixed yearly sum for attendance, and the proprietor naturally took care that his men were well looked after. As a rule—the trade being now stopped—they were *eaten* as prisoners of war in Africa instead of being sold into European service in the islands, where the great majority were well fed, clothed and housed, nursed when ill, and generally cared for. I myself saw a man-of-war chase and capture a slaver; what became of the unfortunate 'emancipated' creatures on board I never knew.

Now look at the treatment the proprietors in the West Indies received. The nation was constantly told the owners were receiving compensation for their loss and that millions had been spent on the price of the slaves, but the landowners derived little good from that. Suppose our farmers in Great Britain had all their horses taken from them at a market price, with a strict prohibition against purchasing others, how could farming be continued? Yet that was the manner in which the unfortunate West Indian proprietor was served; it has constantly been thrown at their heads that they received ample compensation.

I visited Jamaica shortly after the emancipation, expecting from the crusade against slavery I heard of in England to find evidences of the cruel ill-treatment and neglect the poor slaves had received for generations in the bad housing and worn-out condition of the race. How different was everything to what I imagined!

They were still in the homes provided by their late owners: nice little cottages many of these, with gardens attached, having the appearance of our small suburban houses at home, with abundance of fruit-trees, particularly oranges, on which the 'poor slaves' fed their pigs, and as much additional land as they wished to cultivate, which raised abundance of the food they required, with the smallest possible amount of labour. They were not overworked, any more than a farmer overworked his horses, for that would have been to the owners' detriment, and they were a thousand times better off than our own unemployed, or hundreds of the employed, for that matter, in this enlightened twentieth century.

Now look at the aspect from the proprietor's point of view. Things were going on as badly as they could; for the one idea which the antislavery party had impressed on the childlike mind of the negro was that to *work meant slavery*. They simply as a body declined to do any work whatever, and had a high old time of it while the sugar-cane rotted in the fields and the coffee-berries dropped over-ripe from the trees, while the owners of the land were actually starving, and in many instances were forced to abandon their estates, which were left to become a wilderness, as no one would purchase them.

I stayed the greater part of my time in Jamaica with my cousin, the Honourable Duncan Robertson, of Gilnock Hall. His so-called slaves had taken their emancipation, but things went on exactly in the same manner as previously: house-servants, coachmen, grooms, and the whole establishment, continued on precisely the same footing. No locks were on the doors; these stood open day and night, the silver being left on the dining-room sideboard all the time, and the quondam slaves elected to remain where they were perfectly contented and happy.

I should like to record as a fact that only one man was pointed out to me by more than one native as having been flogged; this satisfactorily proved to me that flogging was by no means an everyday occurrence. I should mention that I moved about the island a great deal, so that I am not recording the experience gained in one place or on one estate only. Flogging was the only punishment for serious offences, and I am at a loss to know what other punishment could be inflicted. I am of opinion hooligans would be made the better by the same treatment now.

I had one rather exciting adventure there. Having gone with a young friend to travel on business, we arrived at a sugar estate near Savanna-le-Mar, some two miles from the town, on the second night out. There we found an old gentleman in charge, who was bitter in his complaint that his splendid fields of sugar-cane were rotting in the ground and being devoured by the negroes' pigs, the negroes themselves refusing to do a stroke of work. There was a cartload of sugar-cane standing at the mill, and I proposed, half in fun, that we should grind it ourselves. Off we started, set the mill going, and I began to stuff the canes into the rollers. We had no sooner began than out came the negroes from their settlement, stopped the mill, and *ordered* us back to the house, where we did go, after some lively passages and strong words between the old gentleman and the negroes.

Presently the whole village turned out, men and women, some with axes, some with cutlasses or clubs. Mr. Smith ran into his room and brought out a brace of pistols, one of which he handed to each of us young fellows, retaining a double gun for himself. Rather a steep flight of steps led up to the front-door, and we had just arrived at the head of the steps when the mob arrived at the foot. Old Smith was a plucky old fellow, and called out: 'The first man who puts his foot on these steps will be shot dead, and the second likewise.' This caused a halt, and the women began to use strong language, urging the men to go up and do for us, but no one dared to go first. There we stood, the three of us in a row, and after a time we observed that the crowd began gradually to disperse one at a time. Smith did not seem to take it very seriously, and in due time we had our dinner and retired for the night.

My room was some distance from the others, and Smith had taken his pistols back and hung them in his room. I confess I felt very uncomfortable when I got to my room. Everything was in a dilapidated and worn-out condition. At the end of the room stood a large old-fashioned four-post bed with mosquito curtains. The head of the bed stood against the wall, and was equi-distant from both sides of the room. At the other end, exactly opposite, was a large window without glass, but closed with Venetian blinds in a rather dilapidated condition. I observed also an old rusty sword without a scabbard hanging on a nail on the opposite side of the bed to the door, which was at right angles to the window, and in the far corner of the room.

I soon fell asleep, and how long I slept I know not, but I awoke with a terrible feeling of dread. I partly sat up in the bed and listened, wondering what had wakened me. I observed a single ray of moonlight, coming through the broken window, gleaming across the room, which was in profound darkness. Presently I heard the door being gently pushed open and grating on the floor as it was moved. Then a slight creak on the floor, and then another, evidently a heavy footstep coming towards the bed. The only word which describes my feelings is the word 'horror,' staring as I was towards the door in the profound darkness.

Suddenly a black face, with a large knife in its mouth, appeared for an instant as a man passed through the gleam of moonlight; then I heard breathing close to the side of the bed and the mosquito curtains being gently pulled out, and in another second, they were thrown up. At that moment I sprang with one bound through the curtains on the opposite side of the bed, made a clutch at the rusty sword which, fortunately, I caught, ran round the foot of the bed (all this happened in far less time than it takes to write it), and made a fierce cut in the direction of my would-be murderer. Instead of hitting him I put a big notch in the bedpost, and my adversary ran quickly out of the room and disappeared. The whole thing took place in an incredibly short time and without a word being spoken on either side. I pulled my valise from under my bed and sat on it in the corner of the room till daylight, with the old sword in my hand, being terribly punished by mosquitoes.

Strange as it may appear, it is nevertheless a fact that I did not mention a word of the affair next morning; but I need not say we made the best of our way out of such an unpleasant neighbourhood.

I afterwards went to stay at my own place, Friendship, and found the old housekeeper who had been there in my father's time. Everything was going on comfortably, and everyone was happy. The factor in charge of the estate was a cousin of my own, a Robertson, and he and his elder brother had been taken to Jamaica when young men by my father. The younger brother remained as factor of Friendship, married a black wife, and had a flourishing family. His brother settled at Kingston, and remained a bachelor.

The chief of the Robertsons was at this time in the 42nd Regiment. I well remember seeing him at Blair Atholl games when as a boy I was staying with my aunt, Betsy Stuart, of Fincastle, at the Milton, which she and her sister fortunately had settled on them for life. Like a great many other Perthshire gentry at that time, this chief spent money a good deal faster than it came in from the estate, so to raise money he resolved to sell part of the ancestral property; but, as it was strictly entailed, he had to get the permission of the two next heirs (he had no family himself) to the chieftainship, and it was ascertained, by going back a good many generations, that the legal heirs were my two cousins in Jamaica.

With their permission (they receiving a small sum as compensation) he sold part of the estate. After a time, the same game was repeated, this time for the sale of the whole estate. Permission was again granted, but most fortunately, before any legal document was signed, the chief died, and the old bachelor at Kingston succeeded to the title and estates. Here was a comically sad state of things. The prospective chief of the Robertsons (his nephew) was a delightful black man. I wonder how he would have looked in a kilt! Fortunately, however, the chief married and had a family, and so the black man's nose was put out of joint. Who can say, however, in future generations, that the black man will not succeed should the present direct line fail?

Before leaving Jamaica, I may relate a rather amusing episode which occurred while I was there. My cousin and Mr. Morris were absent on business at Kingston, and I was the only man (?) left at Gilnock. A report was brought in for my absent cousin that some evil-disposed natives were going to loot the house (not our own people). I ought to mention that we had brought out with us from London £500 in silver to pay wages, and most of this was still in the house in boxes of 100 each (these I had taken from Lombard Street in a butcher's cart, and had them driven by a boy all through the slums of East London down to the docks). What a delightful prize if it had only been known to the roughs! Well, to return to my story, the household at night consisted of four maidservants, Mrs. Robertson, and myself. Mrs. Robertson had the silver under her bed, and she took the four maid-servants into her room for the night and barricaded the door.

I had all the rest of the house to myself and a faithful companion— a beautiful Cuban bloodhound named Gift. She could stand on the ground, put her paws on my shoulder, and lick my face. There was a small bit of garden enclosed in front of the house, and a gate leading up to the front-door. My window looked upon this garden, and the house was only one story high. I loaded my rifle and went to bed, Gift lying on the floor. A low, deep growl awoke me, and I jumped up and looked out, the rifle in my hand. The window was without glass—

only a Venetian blind. I saw the gate partly open, and a man crawling forward towards the house. He lay a long time without moving, and I came to the conclusion that he was waiting for others. Presently he came nearer and I covered him with the rifle, and was just about to draw the trigger, when, lo! he put up his head, and turned out to be a black calf!

One day, not long before this. I was out shooting with Gift as my constant companion, when suddenly a wild boar rushed out of some long grass, knocked me over, passing one tusk through my left leg; and before I got on my feet, he wheeled round and made another rush at me. He would certainly have ripped me up, as I was on my back, but Gift seized him fast by the ear and held on. His tusks, as it were, played on her throat, but he could not strike. I jumped up, put my gun to his ribs and drew the trigger, dropping him dead. It was only a very powerful dog that could have held that brute for a moment.

When the negroes were set free, they of course expected to be well paid for any work done, and when paid in copper they smelt it and threw the coin away, calling it a nasty smelly thing. Hence, the £500 in silver had been taken out to pay these delightful creatures.

Jamaica is a lovely country, and I cried when I left it, so happy was I there. We took out a doctor with us who was apparently far gone in consumption. I think he was carried on board. He had come for his health only, and returned after some time perfectly well and strong. I saw him in London after his return, and ascribed his cure entirely to Jamaica. I am sorry I cannot remember his name.

Mr. Morris, having wound up his business, prepared to return home. The ship was then lying at Black River with a full cargo on board.

Mr. Morris embarked, and also a gentleman of the name of Rose, who was coming home with us. The captain and I went on shore, as he had some business to settle, and as all hands were busy getting under way and the pilot on board, we only took two ship's boys to row us ashore. After some little delay we returned to the beach, and great was the indignation of the captain to see his ship beating out to sea, the pilot being afraid that the wind was going to drop. We pulled off as hard as we could, but the ship went faster than we did, and the two boys rowed until they were dead beat, and then gave in. The captain and I then took the oars, and rowed until we were pretty well done. Ultimately the ship condescended to wait for us, and then we got on board. I was terribly exhausted, and within a few hours developed yellow fever.

There being no doctor on board, the captain proceeded, as was the custom in those days, to bleed me in both arms. For some time I was delirious, and quite unconscious of what they were doing with me or to me, but I was told afterwards that I insisted upon having a large poultice of wet salt applied to my spine, and I believe that that saved my life, as it has since been ascertained that saline drinks have marvellous power in cases of yellow fever.

Sometime before leaving Jamaica I had told my cousin that I knew there would be a death on board ship on the way home, and as I had several times had various presentiments which came true, it caused some excitement. After some days of delirium, I must have fallen asleep, for I have a perfect recollection of being awakened by a loud splash. I looked up, and seeing one of the ship's boys sitting at the head of the bed, I said: 'What's that?'

'It was Mr. Rose,' he replied; 'he died last night, and they have just dropped him overboard.'

'Oh, then,' I said, 'I shall recover, for there was only one death to take place on board.'

From that day I rapidly recovered, and I have a lively recollection of the enormous appetite that I developed. No sooner had I eaten a heavy breakfast than I was longing for midday dinner; then just as hungry again for tea, and afterwards for supper. I lay nearly all day on a mattress on deck, and I need not say how kind everyone was to me. I remember also how all my skin peeled off by degrees from the effects of the fever.

THE 3RD KING'S LIGHT DRAGOONS, 1842

CHAPTER 2

Gazetted to the 31st Regiment

We arrived home in due time, and Mr. Morris strongly urged me to give up the sea and go into the army. So, I proceeded to Edinburgh, and went through a course at the Military Academy there, studying military drawing and surveying, and I also became rather an expert both with the rapier and single-stick. I have three medals to show for it.

Mr. Morris then wrote to Lady Clarendon, requesting that she might use her influence to get a commission for a young friend of his. He (Mr. Morris) had for many years transacted all her West India business. Her ladyship kindly wrote a note to Lord Hill, the Commander-in-Chief: 'My dear Lord, I want a commission for a young friend of mine,' giving name, etc., and within a fortnight I was gazetted to the 31st Regiment. This was unusual luck, for most young men in those days had to wait for two or three years with their names on the commander-in chief's list before getting a commission. Years after, when quartered in Ireland, I had the satisfaction of thanking both Lord and Lady Clarendon for their kindness. His lordship was at that time Lord Lieutenant in Dublin.

After the usual six months at the depot at Chatham, I embarked with a draft of recruits for Calcutta early in 1842 to join my regiment, which was then in Afghanistan, avenging the massacre of the 44th Regiment.

On the passage out we had a very disagreeable black man as steward. There was also a cadet on board, who was disliked by everyone on account of his unpleasant manners. The steward's hammock hung in the steerage just outside the cadet's cabin door, and one night, when my chum and I were on watch (as the officers had to keep watch all the voyage), we resolved to have a lark.

The ship was rolling heavily as we proceeded to work, and creeping gently down to the steerage, we tied a string to the steward's hammock, attaching the other end to the cadet's cot; as they swung together with the motion of the ship, it did not awaken either of them. We then put a loose cord over the above-mentioned string, and carried both ends up on deck, when, by jerking the string, we awoke both the parties. The steward growled and made a grab, as he thought, at the person who was shaking his bed, and so found the string, which caused the cadet to sit up in great indignation.

As soon as we had heard the steward was roused, we let go one end of our loose cord, and pulled it up on deck. The result was beyond our fondest anticipation. The steward got noiselessly out of bed and followed the string attached to his hammock, and just as he got up to the cadet's bed to make a grab at the occupant, the cadet hit him fair in the face, knocking him down. A free fight in the dark followed, and we both rushed off to the other end of the ship, and laughed till we cried at the success of our little plan.

Duly arriving at Calcutta, we landed, and were quartered at Fort William.

After a short stay there we started on our march up-country, a battalion of recruits, composed of drafts for the various regiments in Bengal. We used to march on an average twelve miles a day, starting at two or three o'clock in the morning, and finishing our day's work before breakfast, always resting on Sundays or after storms of rain, when the roads became impassable. I generally spent the rest of my day out shooting, but the country in the immediate vicinity of the Grand Trunk Road was very poorly stocked with game.

One day, when out with Dickens, of the 21st Fusiliers, tramping along the high bank of a *nullah*, a native came up to speak to us in a rather excited condition, and requested us to shoot a very large crocodile that had for years lived in a pool below and killed ever so many people, and had become the terror of the women who had to come down the *nullah* for water, sometimes dragging in a cow or a sheep, and not unfrequently a woman or child.

'There he is! there he is!' he said, pointing at a little distance on the other side of the river.

For a long time, I could see nothing, but at last it dawned on me that what I had taken for a log of wood was the brute in question.

'Come,' the native said, 'and I will take you to him.' We kept out of sight, and going up the river about a quarter of a mile, we waded across, and reached the other side.

Presently we came to a place where there were a number of bushes and trees. A well-marked footpath led down through this to the river.

The native pointed to the path in dumb show, indicating that we would find our friend at the other end, but declined to follow us a step further. I had both my barrels loaded with ball, and Dickens the same. I went first, and to prevent making any noise, we both crawled through the bushes on our hands and knees in profound silence. Soon I found myself close to the great brute. He was lying on the sand fast asleep, with just a small bush between me and him.

He was simply a monster. I cannot pretend either to guess his length or his height, as he lay on the sands beside the deep pool of the river; but he appeared to rise over 3 feet from the ground as he lay on his stomach.

I gently nudged Dickens with my elbow, and he replied in a whisper, 'Where?' but that was quite enough to awaken our friend, and I caught his eye glaring at me. He stretched forward one great claw, and disclosed a nice tender spot right under his arm. I put the muzzle of the gun close to this spot, and drew both triggers at once.

Instantly there was a terrific plunge as he bounded into the deep pool. A perfect fountain of water, tinged with blood, burst up, and he disappeared. We waited a long time on the bank of the river in the hope that he might come up again or float. The bubbles, which had risen thickly at first, subsided gradually, but he never appeared. I think he must have been killed, as the two balls were bound to pass through the most vital parts of his body. You might shoot at alligators for years, and never get such a chance of lodging a ball in such a tender place. A number of small tortoises rose to the surface, swam about, and then disappeared, and we reluctantly left the spot.

Everyone has heard of the expert Indian thieves. Our commanding officer was Major Straubenzie (I think of the 39th Foot), whose wife accompanied him, and they had an uncomfortable experience of these fellows.

Our custom was that most of our baggage and some of the servants always moved on in the evening, so as to have breakfast ready on our arrival at camp in the morning. During the night the thieves cleared out everything from Straubenzie's tent, including the whole of the wearing apparel, so that when the bugle sounded the turn-out in the morning, the major and his wife simply could not appear. So, they had to borrow two *doolies* from the doctor, and being rolled up in their bedclothes, were ignominiously carried to the next station.

I need not say that they went well ahead of us, and we knew nothing of the affair till after our arrival in camp.

The only disagreeable experience which I remember having was that one morning, when my servant came in with a candle for me to prepare for the march, as I threw off the bedclothes, I saw to my horror a large cobra nestled quietly for warmth against my naked leg. In an instant he jumped out and disappeared, nearly frightening my servant into a fit.

While we were marching through the Raj Mawl hills, we were warned that there were a number of tigers about, and this we soon found out to be true.

The commanding officer had taken up his quarters in a *dak* bungalow, and you may picture his horror when, just as he was finishing breakfast, he saw a tiger, in broad daylight, pounce upon one of our camp-followers, sit down under a tree immediately in front of the house, and proceed to eat him. He described the steam rising from the unfortunate man's body as the tiger was munching him. As soon as he dared, he sent word down to the camp, and we all turned out, some on the baggage elephants and some on foot. We had a grand tiger-hunt, but of course the tiger was not fool enough to let himself be seen, and so we came back as we went.

But the next day I had rather a disagreeable experience myself. Two of us had been out shooting all day, and when returning to camp, I proposed to fire off my gun, one barrel of which was loaded with ball, as I had no means of extracting it in camp. My companion said: 'Fire at that white mark on the rock there,' which I did. The moment the ball struck the rock, we heard a terrific roar from a tiger close to us. We had a native with us, leading a little dog, and I shall never forget the man's expression. He turned literally blue, owing to the blood leaving his skin, and the dog's hair stood straight on end all over. We made the best of our way back to camp, keeping all close together, and most fortunately Mr. Tiger did not attack or follow us.

As we marched upcountry each detachment was dropped at the nearest point to its own station, and so the battalion gradually dwindled away until we were a mere handful, when, in due time, we arrived at the regiment, which was then encamped near the city of Umballa.

When I joined my regiment at that place, it was armed with flintlocks, and had just returned from the punitive expedition to avenge the loss of the 44th.

When in Afghanistan the general wore a wig, and during the campaign, when they were holding the fortress of Jelalabad, an earthquake occurred, in which the room where the general was asleep came down, smothering him in dust and plaster. So anxious was he to keep up the fiction of wearing his own hair that, when they commenced to dig him out of the ruins, he called out, 'Don't pull my hair!'

Three days after joining the regiment we were ordered off to Kytul. Kytul was what was then called a protected Sikh State, and a compact had been formed with the *rajah* that, at his death, the State was to become part of the East India Company's possessions. The *rajah* having died, his widow, the *ranee*, refused to give up the fort. It was a small town surrounded by a high brick wall, and well-armed. In consequence of this refusal, Sir George Clark, the political agent, resolved to take it by force, so the 31st Regiment, with the 3rd Light Dragoons and some artillery, were ordered to take possession of the place, and Sir George went with us as political agent.

My groom, who was new to the ways of the regiment, did not come up to time with my horse, and there was nothing for it but to march on foot with my company. Presently an officer, seeing me, and learning why I was unmounted, sent me his spare horse. Being a much taller man than myself, his stirrups were too long for me, and as I mounted the animal, he made three bucks, and the third dislodged me, as I had not my feet in the stirrups, and I was landed over his head into a thorn bush. One of the thorns passed right through my cheek and into my tongue. Getting on my feet, I pulled the thorn out and called for the horse, which had been caught, had the stirrups shortened, mounted, and rode the animal for the march. My men were delighted, and murmurs of 'He'll do!' went round.

The horse was a noted buck-jumper, and the senior officer kept me at my distance, as he did not wish it near his own beast, and so I won my spurs with the regiment Kytul was three marches from Umballa, and the third night we camped a short distance from the town. During the night the *ranee* went off with a whole string of carts loaded with treasure, and to distract our attention their soldiers showed themselves—at a respectful distance, however—and as they were armed with matchlocks, kept blowing their matches, as much as to say, 'We are coming.' The consequence was we stood to our arms all night, and the treasure got well ahead. I suppose Sir George did not find this out till the next day, when the whole force went in pursuit; but soon after dark, not having overtaken it, we were halted, piled arms, and lay down to sleep.

I, being very young and foolish, was too proud to bivouac beside the soldiers, so, taking a blanket, I rolled myself well up, head and all, and lay down some yards off. I awoke in the night to a rumbling noise and a violent pull at my hair. This proved to be a wheel of one of our guns, which was passing right along beside my head. It appeared the artillery had come up, and seeing our men asleep, had, in avoiding them, come my way, and another inch or two more and I should have been crushed to death. This cured me of my reserve or pride, and I slept near my own men for the future. We returned to Kytul in the morning.

Sir George Clark had hoped to regain the treasure for the British Government without actually attacking the convoy, as in this latter case part at least of its value must have gone as prize-money to the force. As matters turned out, the whole thing disappeared, and never was seen again, so all the treasure was lost.

We were allowed to enter the walled town of Kytul, but the orders were that nothing was to be taken out. While rummaging in the palace I saw a dagger I greatly coveted, and wrapping the blade in rags, I tied it to my leg, and so passed the searchers. Our uniform then was composed of a pair of white duck trousers and a close-fitting jacket buttoned to the throat, so that the hiding of loot was a difficult matter.

The men had broken the legs off a set of metal chairs and set them up to play at skittles, and after the game left them lying about; one of these was carried away by a soldier, and he afterwards found it was made of solid silver! I have my dagger still.

On returning to Umballa, we heard it was intended to make it a first-class military station. Captain Napier (afterwards Lord Napier of Magdala) was the engineer officer in charge, and he set to work to mark out the cantonment under the real old system. The site was a plain, which had been under crop, and his instrument was a plough. Long lines indicated the main roads, and between them the ground was divided into a gigantic chessboard. Then one fine morning we (the officers) were all marched up from the camp, each to select a square to build on. Napier said:

'Gentlemen, there is your little ground; build a house to your liking on it, and when it is finished you can live in it.'

There were pointed out the field officers' lines, the captains' lines, the subalterns' lines, while at some distance on the other side of the main road the barracks were marked out and planted in echelon.

We were not long in choosing, according to our seniority, our plots, which were a free gift from the government. Each one set to work according to his own ideas. I took care (with a view to brick-making) to choose a piece which was out of favour, owing to its having an old road which had been well churned running through it; this was specially suitable for making the bricks which were to build the walls. Having dug a well, I had water added to make the clay the right consistency; bricks were quickly turned out in uniform sizes by a native from a mould made of wood, and the little native girls carried them off on their heads to dry in the hot sun.

I chummed with another officer, Lieutenant Sparrow; our two plots of ground were thrown into one, and I proceeded to build the house after my own fashion, which consisted of the roof being put on before the walls were begun. A framework of posts with horizontal bars supported the roof, which consisted of split bamboos made into a frame of network, which was then drawn up, lashed on to the supports, and thatched with grass; the walls were soon built in with the dried bricks, manipulated with clay instead of mortar; three glass doors in front and three behind opened off sitting-, bed-, and bath-rooms, and the floors were composed of a sort of asphalt made of mortar and pounded brick.

Before the rains set in, I had finished our house, up to which time we had lived in our tents all the hot weather. So popular was my design that it became the model for many of the subaltern quarters. After we left Umballa I sold it for nearly twice the amount it cost.

Umballa is now one of the largest stations and finest situations in India.

CHAPTER 3

Volunteering to Remain in India

In those days (1843) the 31st Regiment was a grand old corps, having served twenty-three years in India; its commanding officer, Colonel Bolton, had served in the Peninsula. I should be sorry to say how many years of service the two majors had seen, but the junior of them always required a chair to mount his charger, and one of the captains (by no means a senior) had been at Waterloo and proudly wore the medal.

As to the rank and file, many of them had grey hair, and in the ranks, we had the third generation of the 31st. Other men were there who, having come out to the regiment as boys, had their children serving as buglers and bandsmen.

Many of the married women also had been born in the regiment.

Lieutenant E. Lugard had been the adjutant for years, and when he got his company, I was one of his subalterns. As for the quartermaster, he had actually been on board the *Kent*, as also had Lieutenant Bray when a child, whose father was then an officer in the regiment. Everyone must have read Major Macgregor's account of the loss of the *Kent* East Indiaman in the Bay of Biscay. I had the pleasure of meeting Major Macgregor in after-years in Dublin, and his son was the well-known writer under the *nom de plume* of 'Rob Roy.'

Years after, when the regiment returned from India and was quartered at Walmer, in Kent, the captain of the *Cambria*, who rescued the 31st from the *Kent*, came to see us, and, you may depend upon it, received a warm welcome. It was strange to think that the quartermaster, Benson, and Lieutenant Bray, who were there to receive him, had actually been on board his little brig.

To return to India: when I joined the regiment at Umballa, we were expecting the long deferred order for home, but the disturbed state of the Punjab prevented this, and after I had enjoyed only about two or three months' residence in my new house, we were ordered up to Ferozepoor to watch events. There we remained in a standing camp till the beginning of the following hot season, when we returned once more to Umballa, and took possession of our old quarters. We enjoyed the stay at Ferozepoor very much, as there was good shooting then in the neighbourhood; and as we had a pack of foxhounds originally imported from England, we got capital runs with the foxes and jackals.

Most of the hounds had been born in India, and had lost the pluck of their ancestors; but one old hero of the name of Hannibal survived, and invariably had the honour of going in first at the finish. One day the natives brought in a full-grown jackal, having sewn up its mouth with a needle and thread (the native gipsies use this method of securing themselves from the bite of the jackal and other wild animals when they catch them).

I volunteered to carry it off to some distance, and unsew the mouth before letting it start on its run, thus giving it a good chance; this proved more than I could accomplish, for it was a particularly savage animal, and as I placed it on the ground to release its mouth, it rushed up my legs and over my chest, burying its nose in my neck. After I had twice felt the pressure of its cold muzzle there, it occurred to me that were I to let the lips loose the next time it ran up me its teeth would be in my throat, so I was obliged, most unwillingly, to let it go as it was, when he gave the pack a good run before we were in at the death.

While at Ferozepoor I had some of the several marvellous escapes which have followed me through life; over and over again I have been within an ace of losing my life, and been spared by a merciful Providence.

One night a large elephant got savage, broke from its keeper, and started on a furious stampede through the camp. He charged the first tent he came to, which contained twelve sleeping men, tore the canvas down, and trampled it, while the men rolled underneath, inextricably mixed up with tent ropes and pegs; then in a blind fury drove his tusks into the ground with such savage force that one of them broke off short at the jaw, leaving four feet plunged into the ground. Strange to relate, not a man was killed or hurt. More savage than ever with the pain caused by the loss of his tusk, the elephant tore up the main street of the camp, and, fixing his attentions on my tent, kicked out all the pegs on one side.

I, like the men, was sound asleep, and awoke as the cloth of the tent came down on my face; not in the least realising what had happened, I stumbled to my feet in the darkness and scrambled outside, right under the forelegs of the enraged animal, who was standing still, but swaying his body and his trunk backwards and forwards above me. I did not require a second to realize my danger and take the hint to clear off as quickly as possible to the rear of some tents, while the elephant, giving a loud scream, charged on to the horses' picquets and stampeded the frightened animals, with the picquet ropes and pegs dangling behind them, thus causing a terrible disturbance. He was caught soon after by his keepers, no real harm having been done, as no one was hurt.

The following day Captain Brookes had the broken tusk dug out of the ground by his company. It took half a day to do it. It was a fine bit of ivory, and he kept it as a trophy.

One day I was out without my gun and nothing but my riding-whip in my hand, and my favourite dog, Chuffy, was with me, when we fell in with two wolves. I made after and flogged them, expecting they would run, but one turned at once and made a snap at Chuffy's back, just across the loins. Had he caught the dog a little lower down he must have crushed the spine and killed him; as it was, his teeth slipped, and the terrified Chuffy rushed away. I did not see him for twenty-four hours, when he returned covered with mud and dead beat, with four nips or holes where the wolfs teeth had gripped him, fortunately by the skin only. Poor Chuffy had a sadder fate two years after when saving my life from a tiger.

On arrival at Umballa from Ferozepoor, I was suffering from fever, and obtained leave to spend the remainder of the hot weather at Simla, so I set off at once. I shared a bungalow with Lieutenant Willows, Bengal N.I., who came out to India in the same ship with me. Our house was the highest on the hill called Jacko, rising to a great height above the town of Simla, and dotted over with bungalows.

The only other house near us was called the Eagle's Nest, about 100 yards away.

Several of the 31st officers got leave at the same time, and they lived at a large bungalow lower down the hill.

Captains Garvock (afterwards Sir John Garvock) and Longworth, also Lieutenants Hart and Law, were there, and we all enjoyed our stay in the hills immensely, notwithstanding that it was a very wet season. The rain poured down on us through the roof of our house, so that we had to live for two days in bed, the top of which was covered with waterproofs. The whole house was flooded, the water running out at the door. In consequence of the heavy rains, there were several dangerous landslips all over the mountains. An officer was awakened by someone knocking at the door in the middle of the night:

'Please will you take us in?' said a brother officer, with his wife and family; 'our house has just fallen in.'

One night I was awakened by a deep rumbling noise, and I distinctly felt the house shake, but fell asleep again. Fancy my astonishment in the morning to find that a tremendous landslip had just missed our house by a yard or so. It had cut clean through two roads, and great trees had been swept away and smashed up like matchwood. This gave us a long journey up the hill and round the top of the landslip to get down to the town.

Early one morning, before daylight, I saw something through the glass door moving about on the veranda. I got up, and saw that it was a large hyena, carefully snuffing over one of my sleeping servants to see where he could get a comfortable bite. I gave a shout, and the hyena disappeared like a shadow. In the morning, with Chuffy's help, we traced him a good distance into the forest until we came to his den, which was entered by a round hole in the rock, going almost perpendicularly into the ground. I went home, got my gun, loaded both barrels with ball, tied a wax candle to the end of an alpenstock, and, returning to the hyena's den, lighted the candle, and proceeded to wriggle down the hole.

Down, down, I went, sometimes almost faster than I intended, it was so steep. Suddenly I dropped into a large cave, and I could see by the light of the candle bones and skulls scattered about, and the stench was something awful. I could just see at the other end of the cavern a hole which appeared to lead into a second cave, and all at once there was a fearful commotion inside that. To my horror I discovered that it was a whole colony of hyenas just awakened out of their sleep by the flickering of the candle. Had they come out I should have been eaten up in five minutes, and the gun would have been no protection whatever. I need not say that I got back into daylight as fast as possible, and I was thankful to breathe fresh air again. It was no easy task to get out, as I had to work my way with my heels and on my back, always keeping the gun ready and pointed in case of a rush from below; thus, with the gun in one hand and the alpenstock and candle in the other, I had to fight my way up with my elbows and heels only.

One day we made up a party to go fishing for *mahseer* in the interior. So, we started off on horseback—Captain Longworth, Lieutenant Hart (who was Lugard's brother-in-law), and myself. The road to the interior wound round the hills, which were so steep that in a distance of ten miles you could not find a bit of flat ground large enough to pitch a tent. Some parts were beautifully wooded with fine large oaks and pine-trees, others covered with grass, and the road, or rather path, was by no means very safe riding—narrow, with no protection from the steep drop on one side, and in some places the path was only a steep descent of smooth rock, or, at all events, solid rock for the most part. Then occasionally you might meet a troop of hillmen bringing in a large log of wood to Simla; with short cross-sticks under the log, some twenty or more men carried the tree on their shoulders, and this for long distances.

They were delightful people, simple, perfectly honest, bright, and with great natural politeness; but one thing they positively objected to—no European must enter any of their houses. A *rajah* had, however, put up a small hut, a single room about 12 feet square, with a door and no windows, at the place where we were going to fish. Here three of us were stowed away, and, of course, the door was open all night. We had to bring all our food with us, and it was all packed away under a little table in the middle of the hut. Just at daylight something awakened me, and I saw a fox with a round of beef in his mouth, walking out of the door. I shouted, 'Thieves!' jumped out of bed, and rushed after him, followed by the other two, through a stubble field, which punished our poor naked feet terribly. The fox, in getting over the wall at the end of the field, dropped the round of beef, which we picked up in triumph and carried back to the hut.

We used to fish from daybreak until the sun came upon the water, after which time the fish refused to take. We then amused ourselves by fishing in shallow water with a cast-net, as the fish came there to warm themselves in the sun. As the river was muddy, the fish could not see us, so when we cast the net, which was loaded all round with lead, we walked over it with our bare feet, and it was the greatest fun, when we found a big fish in, or rather under, the net, getting him out again, for, of course, we had to kneel down up to the neck in water and grope about till we found him.

We used to start out to fish before daylight, and several times, as we went along the road to where we began fishing, we encountered quite a lot of black snakes crossing the road on their way to the river, but whether to fish or only to drink I cannot say. They passed at a wonderful pace for snakes; we simply stood still and they took no notice of us, and I fancy they returned to the high ground every morning.

Longworth had a native follower, or servant, if you like to call him that, but he was simply a good-natured savage, and had not the slightest idea of the ways or wants of an Englishman. David, as we called him, carried Longworth's rod or anything else as required, generally an umbrella, as the sun in those deep valleys was very powerful. One morning a heavy rain came down, and Longworth shouted for his umbrella. Presently he discovered David squatted on a large stone about 100 yards off, his chin resting on his knees, as only a n——er can squat, and holding up the umbrella quite comfortably. Longworth shouted and David smiled, but did not move till the rain was over, when he politely returned the umbrella!

I forgot to mention that when we came to the place where we had to leave the road the horses were sent back to Simla, and we had to walk the rest of the way. To descend a Himalayan path down a steep hill is about as disagreeable an undertaking as you can well imagine; it is exactly like going down a steep stair four steps at a time, and dropping on each foot alternately. Fancy that sort of work for half an hour or so! The natives go straight up and down the hills, however steep they may be, and nothing but a dog could go with them, and, of course, they have no trousers or shoes to impede them. When we got near the bottom of the valley, we came upon some houses. The inhabitants came out smiling and offered us peaches and walnuts, and there, for the first time, we came upon a native nursery.

On the side of what was to them the public road a small stream of bright sparkling water was conducted, and at a certain spot little jets of water shot out, and under each jet was a very young baby, rolled up so that he could not move, and the water played upon his forehead and ran down behind without wetting his face or clothes. There they slept for hours, perfectly content. I had heard of the water-nurse before on board ship, but I am afraid I did not believe it then. On more than one occasion I passed the place, and the babies were always there, sometimes a proud mother looking on, sometimes no one but the happy babies alone.

About a fortnight after our return to Simla, Hart and I went off by ourselves to another place where we heard there was good fishing. We pitched our tent on a beautiful grassy spot close to the river, and then, by damming up the clear stream which ran past the tent, we made a fine pool for our morning bath. As it was no use fishing after the sun

35

was on the water, we used to enjoy the casting-net, and generally took a snooze in the middle of the day.

I went out on one occasion to shoot by myself, and while crossing the track of a recent landslip (which led right down the river, where there was a raging torrent over the rocks) the ground gave way under my feet, earth, stones, and myself all went sliding down the precipice together, and it seemed as if nothing could save me; but far down below I saw a bush which was still growing, and as I shot past I caught it with my right hand, still keeping the gun in my left. There I held on while the loose earth and stories expended themselves in the river below. I cannot say how long I hung there, but it must have been a long while, as there was no one near at the time, and I had no feeling of pain in my hand, although I was holding on to a cactus bush, the prickles of which were driven into my hand in all directions.

There was a chance of life if I held on, of certain death if I let go; for nothing could have lived in the raging river below me for five minutes, although our fishing water above was comparatively smooth. The natives of the neighbouring village had evidently seen what happened, for I heard great shouts, and presently a band of them arrived at the edge of the landslip, and taking each other's hands they worked their way right across the soft ground step by step, every man carefully putting his feet where the man before him had been. The leading man cautiously made each step firm before he took another. When he came to me and took hold, we returned exactly as they had come, step by step, until we were on solid ground.

Next day Hart wanted to see the place, so we went down along the bank of the river. We very foolishly got on to a rock overhanging the torrent to get a better view, when suddenly Hart slipped and shot off the rock, but I fortunately caught him by the wrist.

Luckily, he was very light and I was strong. I dropped on my knees, and held on to the rock with my toes and the fingers of my right hand, to save us both from being dragged over.

'Oh, save me, save me!' he cried; to which I replied: 'Don't struggle till I get a better grip of the rock with my feet. Never fear; if you go, we'll go together!'

I then gave him my other hand, with which I had been pushing myself back, and got him safely up. Poor fellow! he was killed at the Battle of Moodkee, December 18, 1845, not very long after our little adventure; and his name now appears on the monument which his brother officers put up in Canterbury Cathedral to the men and officers who were killed in the Sutlej campaign.

Hart's leave being up before mine, we just left our tent standing, as it was not worth taking away, and started off one fine morning, he going direct to Simla, while I, all alone, took a wander through the hills with one servant and Chuffy. At some places the natives had not seen a white man for more than a year, and I had to sleep in the open air for the whole fortnight, never being inside a door. I generally stopped at a village or near one for the night, and my bed, a light *charpoy*, was set up in the high road. When I went to the spring or stream to have my morning wash, the whole female population turned out to admire the operation, which was very—trying shall I say?—to my feelings. I generally had a guide from place to place, and ultimately arrived at Sabatoo, and from there returned to Simla.

On my return to Umballa, almost before I got settled in my house, Major Baldwin, Lieutenant Timbrell (the son of a splendid old officer of the Bengal Artillery), and myself, were ordered down to Meerut to take charge of the men of the 40th Regiment who volunteered for the 31st, as all regiments before leaving India were allowed to volunteer for any regiment remaining in India; thus the battalions were filled up with acclimatised soldiers. In the old days our volunteering was very simply conducted. Major Baldwin sat at a table in the orderly-room with a sheet of paper before him, and the men who wished to volunteer were called in one at a time. Then the man's character, as recorded in what was called the *Defaulter Book*, was handed to the major, and he read it. This contained a record of every offence committed since the man enlisted. Then he simply said 'Accepted,' and put the man's name on his paper; or 'Rejected,' when the man walked out, and the next one was called. Thus, any really bad or troublesome men could be 'rejected.' So, it was we got a grand lot of seasoned soldiers with fair characters, and forming nearly half the regiment.

We three, with our volunteers, marched from Meerut to Cawnpore and settled down quietly there, awaiting the arrival of the regiment from Umballa, when one fine morning we got the order to march back again to Umballa, and were several months absent from the regiment.

Timbrell and I did think this rather hard lines, as we had hired a bungalow, made a garden and sunk a well in it for irrigation, and set up a billiard-table; but as orders must be obeyed, we had simply to march back and leave our house and garden behind. On the way back I purchased a boa-constrictor, about 10 feet long, from a party of wandering natives. He was quite tame; I used to hang him round my neck like a fur boa, and he walked about my tent, but the servants were terribly afraid of him.

It was most interesting to see him eat. When I gave him a pigeon—dead, of course—he reared up and struck it hard, seizing it by the head, his two long fangs going through the breast; then he rolled himself round it, crunching all the bones; afterwards he pressed it into his mouth, the under-lip being quite elastic and stretching all round the bird. Thus, holding it in his coil, he pressed it in and took a fresh grip with his fangs, and he worked away till he got it all in, when you could see it quite distinctly passing down into his stomach. The wonderful extension of the under-lip was something I had never seen described in natural-history books. When we marched, I coiled him in a round basket, just as you would coil a rope, put on the lid, and he remained quite comfortable till the day's march was over, when he joined me in my tent. As the native word for a serpent is *saump*, I called him Sammy. Poor Sammy had his head smashed one day, and I could not find out who did it, but that was his end, poor fellow!

CHAPTER 4

The Battle of Moodkee

Things were going from bad to worse in the Punjab. One great man after another was being murdered. The army had got quite out of control, and spoke openly of taking India, and afterwards making a bridge of boats from Calcutta to London. And when an adjutant of one of the regiments (an Englishman) told them that that was impossible, they spat in his face. He told me that himself when we were first quartered at Lahore, on the termination of the first great Sikh War. The Sikh Army for that campaign was composed of old and well-tried veterans, who had never been beaten; and who does not know now what splendid fighting material the Sikhs are made of? This we found out to our cost, when we met them face to face in the Sutlej campaign, which only lasted six weeks, and in that short time we lost 10 officers and 203 non-commissioned officers and men, 16 officers wounded, and a like proportion of men. I am sorry I cannot give the exact number of wounded, but only four of us officers came through scatheless, and I was one of the four.

But to proceed with the thread of my story. On our arriving finally at Umballa, we found that our colonel's son (Bolton) had been appointed adjutant of the 31st, being transferred from another regiment to ours, and had succeeded Lugard in that appointment, the latter having been promoted to captain.

Bolton had a great taste for private theatricals, and got a house in the lines handed over to us to convert into a theatre. I was immediately installed as scene-painter and stage-manager, and was also the first lady of the company. Mrs. Neland, a sergeant's wife, was my dresser, and had very good taste, and for the next three months it was a never-ending source of amusement learning our parts, rehearsing, and acting. A young officer just out from home was the other lady of our company. He was small and very good-looking, Tritton by name, and did the smart young ladies who had to be made love to, while I was sometimes young and sometimes old, with the assistance of a burnt cork to mark the lines of age. We had all sorts of comical adventures.

In one play I came on as a young lady leading a pet dog by a scarlet ribbon. Lieutenant Bray was my lover. He walked gracefully forward, exclaiming 'Dearest Susan,' and threw himself into an attitude of devotion, when my pet dog pinned him by the calf of the leg, and his speech ended in a yell of pain, to the huge delight of the audience, who roared till their tears ran down. One other adventure will suffice. Lieutenant ——— had to be discovered (as the curtain went up) in the centre of the stage, dressed as a lady and about to sing. The curtain had to be rolled up from the bottom by two men at the side (out of sight, of course). The bell rang, and up went the curtain, catching the lady's (?) dress. She seized the curtain, and struggled to force it down.

Another tug from the men—quite unaware why the curtain would not go up—when up went the poor lady, hanging on and kicking frantically. What all the audience saw was a pair of legs kicking wildly up and down two or three times, till the curtain finally went down with a bang and the petticoats were released. Of course, these little incidents were quite as much amusement to the audience as the play, knowing as they did who the actors were.

Meanwhile the troops were being moved upcountry, and the commander-in-chief, Sir Hugh (afterwards Lord) Gough, arrived at Umballa; also, the governor-general, Lord Hardinge, his son, and his staff, and with him came the Crown Prince of Prussia (this prince never came to the throne), with an *aide-de-camp* and doctor. We had a grand performance in our little theatre, and the crown prince was very much fascinated by the appearance of one of the ladies, and requested to be introduced to her.

On being told that the lady in question was an officer, he refused to believe it, and insisted upon seeing her. He was highly amused when he came to dine next day at our mess, and I was presented to him, and had the honour of taking wine with him as Miss So-and-so of the night before!

Not long after this the news came that the Sikhs had invaded India, and were marching south. Wild excitement was the order of the day, and every available man was hurried up to the front by the commander-in-chief.

We, the 31st, marched from Umballa, as fine and fit a regiment as ever stood on parade, 1,200 strong. What orders the colonel got I know not, but he hurried us on night and day without waiting for our baggage or mess.

The first day's march went on till darkness closed in, when we lay down on the ground, having had nothing to eat all day since breakfast. We slept till daylight next morning, when we were again hurried forward, halting in a short time near a large village. We had no sooner piled arms than I and others went off to forage. We merely wanted food; we did not plunder or do any harm to the inhabitants. The first thing I got hold of was a large *chatty* holding about a gallon of fresh milk.

Immediately after, I met one of my own men coming out with an armful of hot *chupatties*.

'Hulloa,' I said, 'where did you get these?'

'Oh.' he said, 'an old fellow in there has just been making them for me.'

So, we sat down together. He got half the milk, and I shared his booty.

Lieutenant Atty had an adventure that pained him very much. He went into the village and took out a *chatty* that was lying in a corner full of grain to feed his horse. What was his surprise to find, when he poured it out to fill the horse's nosebag, a beautiful pair of gold bangles hidden in the grain. Some poor woman, expecting to be robbed, had taken them off and placed them there for safety, and so she lost her bangles altogether, as there was no time to go back with them; no Britisher would have taken them from her wrists had she left them there.

The next morning early, we pushed on as hard as ever, and my food for that day consisted of a large lump of brown sugar and half the contents of my horse's nose-bag. That night I was so done up that I simply lay down where we halted, and fell fast asleep as I lay on the sand, with my chum, Timbrell, beside me. In the morning we heard that the mess-sergeant had hurried up on an elephant during the night with a small supply of cooked food, which was carefully divided amongst the officers. A piece of tongue was cut in two and laid aside for myself and Timbrell, but it had disappeared in the morning. Afterwards, Ensign P. confessed that he was so hungry that he had eaten it all. He never heard the last of that performance, and years after he was received with a shout of 'Who stole the tongue?' Timbrell and I were not guilty of this, but some of the others thought it rather fun to chaff him.

The last day's march, which culminated in the Battle of Moodkee,

The First Sikh War Theatre

will always remain strongly impressed upon my mind, as that was my first experience of the whistle of a bullet fired in anger.

Just at the break of day the colonel halted the regiment, and gave the word of command in a loud voice: 'With ball cartridge, load.'

I may mention at this time that we were quite alone, with no other troops near us, as far as I knew.

Then he turned to me and said, pointing to a village about half a mile off: 'Robertson, take a corporal and two men, and see if the enemy are in that village.'

'Pleasant,' thought I, 'for our small party, as, if they are there, small chance of our coming back again!' Fortunately, they were not in that locality, and so we marched on.

The colonel appeared in a perfect fever to get forward, and as we hurried on the men kept falling out from sheer fatigue.

Soon we found ourselves a mere handful, and had to halt for some hours until the men slowly crawled up one by one.

Colonel Bolton was a fine old soldier, but very strict, and still adhered to ancient ways and customs. In those days the men had to wear high and stiff leather stocks to keep their heads up, about as absurd an article as can be imagined for a man to fight in. On this occasion he, the colonel, was quite wild at the straggling of the men (as if they could help being done up, poor fellows!), and he observed one of them with his stock off. 'What do you mean, sir?' he said. 'Put on your stock immediately.' I was standing close to the man, and observed a wild expression come over his worn face.

For a moment I thought he was going to shoot the colonel; then he put his forehead on the muzzle of his firelock, and blew his brains out. I don't know how the colonel felt, but it gave me a very ugly turn. The body was gently put into a *doolie*, and on we marched again till late in the afternoon, when we halted. Throwing myself down on the sand, I said to a brother officer: 'I could not march another yard to save my life.' We had now overtaken the headquarters of the army, and we saw other regiments about, but, as far as I know, received no orders from anyone in authority.

Suddenly the alarm sounded, and we struggled on to our feet. Our general was Sir Harry Smith, commanding the first division, in which we were. Probably he did not know that we had arrived, as we had received no orders whatever, and at this time I did not know who was to be our general or where we were going—in fact, we knew nothing whatever but that we had been pushed forward day and night.

However, the colonel gave the order, 'Fall in, quick march,' and we trotted on about a mile till we came in sight of a great line of jungle. Then we halted and formed line, with all the precision of a parade, the men being dressed in perfect parade order. I was the senior subaltern of No. 1 Company, which was commanded by Captain Wills, and little Tritton was the ensign.

Just as the line was formed, facing full upon the immense extent of thick jungle, *ping* came a bullet just over my company, and an Irishman in front of me exclaimed, 'Holy Jasus! that was a bullet!'

Then the word of command was given, 'Quick march.' and we advanced straight down on the jungle, which extended right in front of us. When within a few yards, I heard the colonel call out, 'Level low, men—level low!' but almost before they got their muskets to their shoulders, we received a withering volley from the unseen enemy at close quarters, making a terrible number of gaps in the line. Down went the colonel and his horse and the bugler at his side, all three shot.

The men gave a wild Irish yell, and rushed into the jungle, where a desperate hand-to-hand fight took place. Immediately the regiment was entirely broken up in utter confusion.

No words of command were given—indeed, none would have been heard if given; but each officer, followed by a mob of his men, was fighting on his own hook. My pay-sergeant came up to me immediately after the first volley and said: 'The captain is killed, sir; you are in command of the company.' It is impossible to describe how the fight went on, but the one idea seemed to be to drive the enemy out of the jungle at the further side. As I was moving forward, I passed a tree, behind which a Sikh officer was standing. I did not see him, but he made a fair cut to take off my head. At the same instant Lieutenant Pollard, who was immediately behind me, put up his sword over my head and caught the blow, but received a cut in the shoulder himself. Just at that moment a grenadier drove his bayonet into the Sikh and drew his trigger. The Sikh fell right in front of me, and I stepped over him. The whole thing was done so instantaneously that I knew nothing of it until Pollard told me after the fight was over.

The next instant, I remember, I saw Captain Napier (afterwards Lord Napier of Magdala), riding all alone, dressed in plain clothes, and having nothing but a walking-stick in his hand. Then I saw several of the enemy rush at him, a cloud of smoke obscured my view, and I saw no more; I reported afterwards that I had seen him killed, but, wonderful to relate, he had escaped unhurt.

SIKH WARRIORS

I very much regretted afterwards that I had not asked him for particulars of the adventure.

I understood that he rode all the way up from Umballa alone, and had just arrived in the middle of the fight, riding straight into the battle.

Soon I found myself out of the jungle on the other side, with one of the men hanging on to my hand, exclaiming: 'Come back, sir—come back! Look where we are!' And sure enough, there we were, right behind one of the enemy's batteries, which was blazing away at our own people. The gunners were too busy to notice us.

I cannot say how time flew, or where we went, or what we did, but the next thing I remember is that we were running right up against the commander-in-chief and his staff, while Lieutenant Law, of my own regiment, was wildly waving his sword about and shouting, 'Charge! charge!' Sir Hugh Gough then called out in a loud voice, 'These guns must be taken!'

I ran up to him, caught him by the knee, and cried out, 'Where are the guns, and we will soon take them?'

Young Fitzroy Somerset, one of the staff, heard what I said, took off his cocked hat, put it on the end of his sword, held it up, and called out: 'Follow me, and I will show you the guns.'

We rushed after him with a loud cheer and took the guns, bayoneting the gunners, who fought desperately to the last man. If I am not mistaken, these were my old friends whom I had been behind when emerging from the jungle shortly before.

It was now getting dark; the enemy had evidently retired, for the firing had almost ceased.

Trotting along with my little mob of men behind me, I ran up against a brother officer, Lieutenant Elmslie, who also had a small company following him. Elmslie remarked to me: 'What a terrible lot of our poor fellows are killed!' At that moment a Sikh, who was sitting in a small tree just over our heads, took a deliberate shot at us, and the ball passed within an inch between our faces. Instantly every one of our parties levelled and fired at him, and down he came, just at our feet, riddled with bullets. This was the Battle of Moodkee, 1845.

In this battle, as in all the others in which the Sikhs were our adversaries, their gunners were conspicuous for their reckless bravery and devotion to their guns. They never left them, but died rather than yield; and there were no white flags and no quarter asked or given on either side, so we had just to fight it out.

46

THE 31ST AT THE BATTLE OF MOODKEE, 18TH DECEMBER, 1845

Shortly after my return home I received a letter from Lieutenant
Bray, a brother officer (who was home on sick leave at the time of the
war), asking me to write an account of the campaign, which I did.
He afterwards returned my letters, saying, 'You ought to keep these:
they give such a clear idea of what took place'; and, as I still have the
originals, I take the liberty of publishing them, even if there is some
slight repetition:

Braendam, by Stirling,
November 7, 1846.

My Dear Bray,

I received your long letter of questions the very night I left
London for Scotland, and had the pleasure of answering it in
prospect for the voyage down, but I was so sick that I could do
nothing but confound steamboats in general, and the one I was
in in particular. We were sixty hours on the passage in a gale
of wind.

I am now on leave till the return of the regiment, when I hope
you will come and see all your old friends that are left of us.

What will please you best, I suppose, is an account of all the
uprisings and downfallings of the 31st from the 12th December, when we left Umballa, up to the end of the campaign, so
I shall give you my own ideas on the subject, such as they are.
We got the order on the 10th to march on the 12th towards
Ferozepoor, and most of us had no carriage, as *unts*, (camels),
and *hackeries* were not to be had for money, so we got them for
"love," 'tis said, but Mrs. ——, the commissariat humbug's wife,
knows best.

The morning we marched Bolton gave me leave for a few
hours to look for "carriage," so I charged at the first *hackery* I
saw, and took it by force, after a great fight with three *gomashtas*
(chief natives of commissariat), of Mr. Simpson's establishment.
The line of march was a scene of the greatest confusion, and no
end of smashes, the *unts* being *burra, bobery, wallas*. Lots of *hackeries* were stuck in the sand, with very little chance of getting
out again, and the n——rs, of course, having a quiet smoke on
the carpet of patience, while the *hackery walla* twisted the *biles'*
(bullocks) tails, even to cracking, and shouted, "*Hack, hack!*" I
saw a camel jammed tight into a ditch, with all the soldiers'
tin pots squashed; one soldier was trying to pull it up by the

tail, two others punched its head with their muskets, and the n——r tugged at the peg in its nose from the front. A little to the right two or three camels were going at full gallop, with the men's bedding flying off in all directions.

Some of us had our things on *tats*, or horses, and others had nothing but *coolies*. I got to camp at the end of an eighteen-mile march, and found the mess-tent just pitching, but nothing to eat in camp, as the *consama*, (messmen), had agreed to supply us with a breakfast mess; and no one had anything to eat except old Willes, who was laughing at us all, as he had refused to join the breakfast mess. That day we had nothing to eat except gram or n——rs' cold *chupatties*. I did not see my baggage till next morning, and slept in Captain Willes' tent on the ground, and was *very* cold. I hugged old Carlo most affectionately to keep myself warm. The next day we went two marches on to Sirhind, and then to the *dak* bungalow, where we left the Ludhiana Road and took across country to Busean in two days, and then two other marches to the village of Moodkee, about three o'clock on the afternoon of the 18th.

On the 17th I had nothing to eat; we got into camp after dark at night, and I fell fast asleep on the sand, and did not move till the bugle sounded in the morning. There was a little bit of bread and beef served out at the mess-tent to each officer, and P. stole a tongue which was to be divided among those who were absent. We did not find out till long after who had taken it, but we used to shout out at breakfast, "Who stole the tongue?" And at length P. confessed, saying that someone else would have taken it if he had not! This brought the whole mess about his ears, and some never gave him a moment's peace afterwards; he has since bolted to the 65th, I think.

On the 18th, about twelve o'clock, I got some *chupatties* and milk out of a village, which we looted to a small extent, but only for grub; the *sepoys* took all they could get, and forced open doors and windows wherever they went—the *sewars!* (pigs). We were regularly done up when we got into camp at Moodkee, and lay down on the ground to sleep, as the tents were not up. I was just dozing off when I heard a running of men and the order to fall in sharp. We formed at quarter distance column and went forward immediately, some of the officers with their swords drawn without the belts, and the men with their jackets

49

off. Old Quigley of the grenadiers was dressed this way. You may remember him as one of the oldest 31st men. Forward we went, no one knew where to, but all the other regiments were doing the same. Presently the artillery began to blaze away ahead of us, and we saw the shells bursting in the air. We all forgot sore feet then, and went on at a kind of run for about three miles, the men calling out, "Come on, boys, or they will be away before we get at them."

Old Willes was riding his white charger, as he was quite done up and couldn't walk. Tritton and I were his subs. We deployed into line, a short distance from a low, thick jungle, on the other side of which there were lots of dust, smoke, and what the men called "A —— row going on." Just as No. 1 was formed something hit the dust in front of us and went whiz over my head. One of the men called out, "Holy Jasus! that was a bullet!" It was the first I had heard, and sounded very nasty.

We moved forward with lots of *sepoy* regiments behind us, and the 80th on our left. Presently I saw them form square and some cavalry come out of the dust. This proved to be a few of the 3rd Light Dragoons, who had been separated in the confusion from the regiment. Two or three of them halted close behind me, and one called out, "Go on, boys; there are lots of them before you." We were through them from right to left. The man was plastered with dirt, and his sword bloodstained. On we went into the jungle, with a tremendous fire of musketry and guns in front of us. Of course, we were much broken by the bushes, which would have done well for Light Infantry, but for nothing else, and the men were beginning to get hit. The first person I saw on the ground was Bulkeley, who looked quite dead, and just then there was a sort of rush to the rear of a chief and his followers on horseback, who had been with us all the morning to show us the shortest way. How he got into the fight I know not, but he made the best of his way out again. A "beast" with two *tom-toms*, who had tormented us all the day with his thumping, nearly rode over us. He was followed by the *hooka burda*, (man who carries *hooka*), standard-bearer and the *bie logue*, (his companion), in a terrible hurry. The *sepoys* were doing the same, and one was shot by our men for running away. I saw a batch of them behind a big tree, firing straight up in the air, and shouting to us, "*Barrow*, ('Go on!'), *Broders, barrow!*" But no "*Barrow*" in them! The last words I heard Bolton say were "Steady, 31st—steady, and fire low for your lives!" Cockins, the bugler, was trying to hold the grey horse, when they were all three hit and went down together. This was from the first volley by the enemy. Shortly after Willes was hit, and I took command of No. 1 (which I had all through the campaign). The ball entered his right arm, below the shoulder, and went into his chest, making only one wound. He said he was hit from behind by the *sepoys*. Young was hit in the back of the neck, and the buckle of his stock saved him, as the ball ran round and came out in front. Hart and Brenchly were both hit in the body, and did not live long.

We soon got into a regular mob, blazing away at everything in front of us, and nearly as many shots coming from behind as in front. I saw Napier, the Umballa "Wattle and dab" man, (referring to his powers as house-builder at Umballa), in a blue pea-coat and black sailor's hat, laying about him, and Sir H. Hardinge in a black coat and "tile" with his "star" on. Sir Hugh Gough rode up to us and called out, "*We must take those guns!*" Law was standing near me with his legs wide, shouting out, "Charge! charge!" and hitting the ground with his sword, and sometimes the men's toes (just as he used to set Growler on Shaw's dog). I called out to Sir Hugh Gough: "Where are the guns, and we will soon take them?" and Somerset put his hat on his sword, and called out, "Thirty-first, follow me!" We rushed after him through the smoke, and had the guns in a moment.

On we went, and came upon two light guns which the enemy were trying to take off the field; but some of our shots hit the horses, and brought them to a stand. They then took a shot at us, not twenty yards off; down we went on our noses at the flash, and the grape went over our heads in a shower. I felt it warm; then a rush, and the guns were ours, the gunners not attempting to run away, but cutting at us with their *tulwars*. I think those two guns were taken away by the Sikhs later on that night, as I never saw them afterwards. Pollard was shot in the leg at Moodkee, and the sergeant-major, old Mulligan, was cut all to pieces. After it was quite dark the firing was kept up, the men blazing away at nothing, or at each other, and the bugles sounding "Cease firing" in all directions.

At last they left off firing, and we got something like a regiment formed at quarter distance, but no colours or bugler to sound the regimental call, so we got a n———r bugler to try it, and just as he got out a squeak someone nearly knocked the bugle down his throat; and this was Sir Harry Smith, who asked what on earth we were making such a row for. We were a long time collecting the men, and then marched back towards camp, but were halted some way in front of it, and had to sleep on the sand till morning. So much for my first battle. If you would like to have the others, let me know, and you shall have them the first wet day I am at home.

The other letter was dated November 27, 1846, and it must be remembered these letters were not written for publication, and in the familiar style of one brother officer writing to another. I may state that years after this date, when Bray had left the 31st Regiment, we used often to have a chat about old times at the Rag in London. He, I know, served throughout the Abyssinian campaign under Lord Napier of Magdala. I have already mentioned that Bray (when a child) was on board the *Kent*, East Indiaman, which was burnt in the Bay of Biscay. His father was an officer in the 31st., and afterwards, I believe, commanded the 39th in India.

My Dear Bray,

I had the pleasure of receiving yours in answer to my last, but have been moving so much about from one place to another lately that I could not find a quiet day to give you more of the army of the Sutledge, not Sutlej, as they make it now.

The morning after Moodkee, volunteers were called for to bring in the dead and wounded, and White and I went out with a party of men. We had scarcely got to the field when the commander-in-chief ordered us in again, saying that the Sikhs were advancing upon us. I got leave from White to go and look at them, and after riding a little way I saw the camp-followers running like mad; the *doolie*-bearers dropped the *doolies*, and, making a grab at their *lotas*, (brass drinking-vessels), and *copra*, (clothing), bolted.

Two or three elephants, loaded with dead, were running as fast as the *mahouts*, by screaming and kicking, could make them go, and one of our sergeants was hanging on to an elephant's tail, not having had time to get up before the stampede. Presently I saw the Sikh cavalry coming up at a gallop, with Lall Singh at their head. I just took a good look at them, and then cut back as hard as I could. I found the regiment formed in front of the camp, and ready to move forward; but we only stood in the sun all day, and then went into our tents in the afternoon, and in the evening buried poor Hart and Brenchly in one grave, below a large tree on the west side of the village of Moodkee.

The next day we had a rest, and some more troops joined us from the rear.

The following day, being the 21st, we turned out at two in the morning and moved forwards towards Ferozesha. We marched all day in a sort of letter **S** direction, without water, and in the afternoon, when the troops were quite done up, formed in order of battle. Sir Hugh, having found out on which side of the Sikh camp their batteries were, of course went in front of them, and having sent forward a few 6-pounders, to let them know where we were, and get ready, we moved forward; and there being plenty of jungle and bushes, of course, Light Infantry were not wanted, and we formed two fine long lines to catch all the shot as they came! The 6-pounders finding no go, Sir Hugh ordered the Cavalry to charge the camp, which was done in the most splendid style by the 3rd Dragoons *alone*. Our N———r Cavalry, I believe, did not support them in any way, and their commander's (Captain B. Melville) defence was: "Finding that the enemy had moved off, we made for Ferozepoor!"

The 3rd Dragoons, after cutting their way through many thousand Sikhs of all arms, and taking a number of guns, but not being supported in any way, were obliged to make the best of their way out of the camp with great loss; and, having no spikes, the guns which they had taken were immediately reopened upon them. The infantry were all this time blazing away, and the Sikhs giving us round shot, shells, grape, and canister, for our musket balls, the first line gradually advancing, and we, moving after them, got most preciously peppered without firing a shot. We now found the ground covered with men of the 80th, 29th, and 1st Europeans, and they kept calling out, "Don't fire, boys; our men are in front of you."

It was now getting dark, and we got the order to move forward, and a little way on we formed a complete line of men and muskets on the ground, with here and there a man or officer standing, or on one knee, keeping up a fire as well as they could, our men calling out, "Give them it now, there is nothing but the Sikhs in front of us." Just then a shell burst in my company and knocked a lot of us down. I thought it was all over with me, but got up and found I was not hurt. About twenty men were smashed, and some appeared to have been blown two or three yards off their feet. Baldwin was a little to my left, behind No. 2, and I heard him call out, just as if on parade, "Captain White, keep your men together, sir, and fill up that gap!" And immediately after, he said, "I am hit, men; take me off!" One of the men caught him as he fell, and he was taken to the rear. Poor Bernard was shot about the same time, quite dead. His sword was brought to me by Sergeant Kelly, No. 1, and I told him to keep it. The next day Noel took it, as he had broken his own in the final charge. We stood our ground and kept up a sharp fire for a long time, every now and then advancing a little till we were close up to the entrenchments. Many of their tents were on fire, and by that light I saw a large gun, just in front of us, and not a man left with it. The Sikhs had retired, and we had possession of this part of their camp; but instead of holding what we had got with so much loss, we were ordered to retire for the night.

We then went back in a sort of mob, men of all regiments being mixed together, and every officer shouting for his own company or regiment. One man would say, "Where is the 80th?" "Here it is," would say another. "No, this is the 31st," said a third, and so on. The colours of two or three regiments were all together, and everyone would have it he was right. I ran up against Law, who was crying out, "Where is Paul and the colours?" and at last, seeing him, he held on, and called out, "Here is the 31st; this way, 31st," etc., till we got into some sort of order. But there was no firing in front of us then, and we thought the battle was over. We formed at quarter-distance column, and lay down on the cold sand. It was then we began to feel the most frightful thirst, and not a drop of anything was to be had. I had a little gin in a flask, and took a pull at it, giving the rest to the men with me. But this only made us the worse, and the cold was so intense that we were quite frozen.

I shall never forget the miseries of that night. There was no end of a row in the Sikh camp and a constant dropping fire, but we thought this was our own people, and by the light of the tents

I could see there were lots of men moving about, and presently one or two guns opened on us with grape and round shot. We just lay where we were and let them pepper away. There was a horrid bugler sounding some n———r regimental call, and every time he sounded, *bang! bang!* came the grape amongst us. At length Sir Hugh, who was just behind us with those of his staff who were left ordered the 80th to form line and retake the guns. It was just as well he did this, for they had not gone far before they met an immense number of Sikh infantry crawling down upon us, to find out where we were.

After a sharp fire, and losing a section of Grenadiers by one discharge of grape, they took the guns, and I am not sure but they had to take them twice during the night, having nothing to spike them with. The cold was very severe, and we had nothing to cover ourselves with, so I took little Tritton in my arms and put Sergeant Murphy at my back, with two or three fat men for blankets and pillow, and there we lay all night, one above the other, to try and keep ourselves warm. I was soon fast asleep, for even the shot could not keep me awake.

A little before daylight we stood to our arms and formed line with the artillery in front of us, but Colonel Spence, with great judgment, gave, "Threes, left shoulders, forward," and got clear of the artillery to the right. There was a thick mist and you could only see a few yards. Presently a battery opened in front of our artillery, and they answered; if we had been behind them, we should have been well pounded. We advanced very quietly upon a strong battery on the left of the Sikh camp and just at the angle; they did not see us till we were right upon them, and they had only time to fire one or two rounds when we gave them a volley and charged right into them. Spence was on foot in front and was one of the first over the ditch. We bayoneted a great many artillerymen and infantry who stood to the last; we also took a standard, and then charged on through the camp, polishing off all we could get at.

I got a drink out of a gun-bucket, the water being as black as ink, and my throat was in such a state with the want of water that it cut me like a knife. As we passed through the camp, I got some gram and a lump of *goor* (rough sugar), upon which I breakfasted. We formed a sort of irregular line of all the regiments on the other side of the Sikh camp, and Sir Hugh Gough and Sir H. Hardinge rode down the line, and there was great cheering. Law was reported shot, and I took command of the Grenadiers, and gave Tritton No. 1. When the Big Wigs came to the 31st, I was on the right of the line with a Sikh *tulwar* in one hand and a lump of *goor* in the other, grubbing as hard as I could. We were told to send an officer and party to get water, and I went to see what was to be had in the camp.

I found Law doing the same; he, being an old hand at looting, had left us the moment the fight was over, and I made up my mind to do the same the next time. This is the end of the second battle, but the Sikhs came back and fought another the same day, which I shall give you in my next. Let me have a line when you get this with any remarks you may think necessary.

Pollard was mounted on the evening of the 21st repeating the words of command (for the colonel, who had almost lost his voice), and was shot through the body, but lived till the 24th. Pilkington was shot through both ankles the same night, but I did not see either of them.

No word of the regiment yet. I do wish they were home.

Trusting that this will find you well,

     Believe me, my dear Bray,

        Yours very sincerely,

               J. P. Robertson.

I am much afraid that our casualties at Moodkee were very much increased by some regiments of *sepoys* who remained outside the jungle, and blazed away, hitting friends and foes alike, while the fight was going on, as early in the morning when we were looking for the wounded and removing the killed, I did not see a single dead *sepoy*. Fortunately, they fired very high, as men will do when much excited. Captain Young, as I said before, was hit fair on the buckle of his stock from behind.

CHAPTER 5

The Battle of Aliwal

The 31st Regiment came out of the campaign with only four officers unwounded, and who had been in every action. The four were Major Spence, the biggest man in the regiment, Captain Longworth, the tallest, and Lieutenant Noel and myself. In every action we had to march straight up to the enemy's guns and take them. Sir Hugh Gough's simple strategy was to put the strongest regiment into the hottest place, and no attempt was ever made to outflank or turn a position, which must account for the heavy list of casualties.

At daylight the major called for volunteers to look for the wounded men. Captain White and I offered ourselves at once, and with the assistance of some elephants we accomplished our painful task.

After two days' rest the army advanced in the direction of Ferozesha. I was on the rear-guard, and was particularly struck, while darkness lasted, with the terribly circuitous route we were taking, as I could tell this by the stars.

Here is Major Spence's account of his experiences in the campaign:

I appear to have had a charmed life, commanding as I did the regiment in every action, and have escaped being wounded in a most astonishing way. Had two horses killed under me, balls through my cap and scabbard; my sword broken in my hand by grape-shot, and at Sobraon a Sikh, who was lying apparently dead in the trenches, jumped up, when my head was turned the other way, and was bayoneted by one of my men just in time to save my life; I having just broken my sword in an encounter.

My own escapes will come in in their own place. Some of the wounds were remarkable. My own captain, Wills, was hit on the right arm about half-way between the shoulder and elbow. All that was to be seen was a red spot, not even bleeding, and the ball had entered there, ran up his arm, and down into his lungs. After the fighting was over at Ferozesha, the wounded from Moodkee were brought up to the regiment (as we lay on the ground) as they were passing on to the hospitals at Ferozepoor. Captain Wills, who was quite sensible, made the *doolie*-bearers bring him to his own company, and it was then that I saw the wound. When I went to him, he said in a low weak voice, 'Don't let them take me away. Let me die with my company.' But what could we do with a dying man in the fighting-line; so he had to go, poor fellow! but more than one eye was wet as we saw him carried away. He lived only a day or two. It is little scenes like these that we seldom hear of in the glowing accounts of glorious victories.

At Ferozesha, Lieutenant Flasket was hit on the heel of his boot, and his foot wrenched right round, and it was many a day before he put it on the ground again. I carried him on my back for some distance, as we were only being pelted at long range by the enemy. As I said, I was one of the rear-guard leaving Moodkee, and it was late in the afternoon before we joined the regiment, which was almost immediately ordered to advance, and the enemy's guns opened on us at long range. The balls at first came popping past just like cricket-balls at play. Then an ugly shot came whiz, and hit my right-hand man fair in the face, and I heard a man exclaim, 'There's poor Finnigan down!' That was the first casualty I saw; but presently our guns opened, and the firing became loud and fierce. We simply stood and saw nothing in front of us for the smoke, but loaded and fired away as hard as we could. Major Baldwin was on horseback just behind me, when he called out (but quite quietly), 'I'm hit, men; take me off.' Poor fellow! that was his death-wound, and we never saw him again.

Suddenly, just in the rear of my company, a shell exploded, and I and three other men were thrown violently on our faces. I thought I was killed, and wondered that I felt no pain; then I moved my arms and they were all right, and I got up quite unhurt. But I shall never forget the man lying just in front of me, partly on one side, and in the exact attitude of the celebrated statue of the dying gladiator on his shield. His face was quite calm, and without saying a word he rolled over dead in a moment. The fighting went on till quite dark, when we were ordered to retire a short distance and lie down; and what a memorable night it was, with our damp clothes and the thermometer below freezing-point, and a fierce burning thirst, and not a drop of

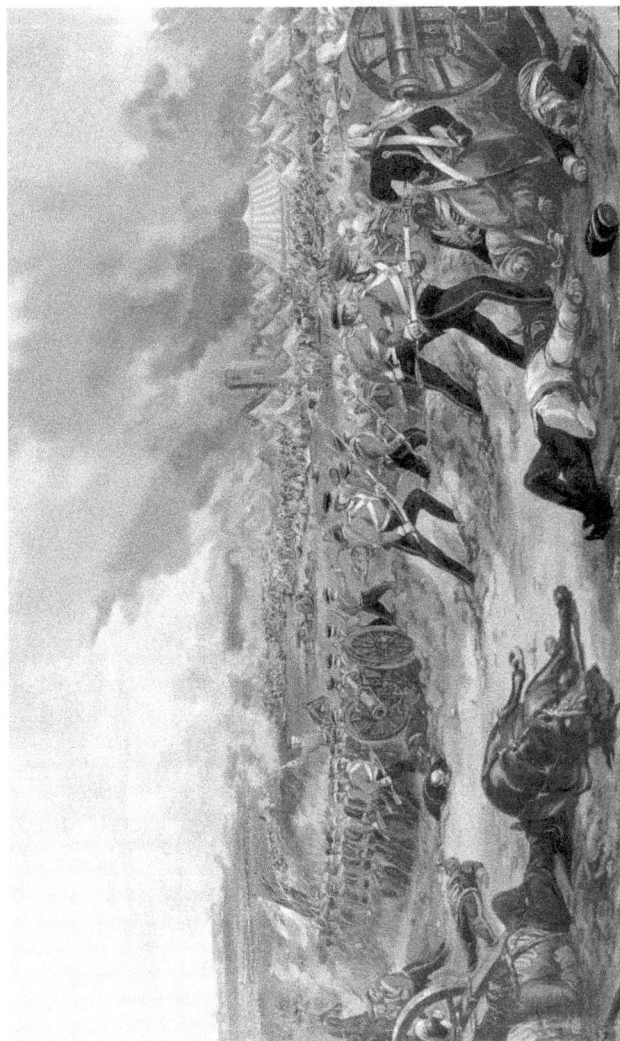

The Battle of Ferozeshah, 21st & 22nd December, 1845

water to be had. We lay there all night, and I was almost frozen to death—very wonderful, but quite true. I fell asleep huddled up with a private on each side in the vain hope of getting a little warmth. I dreamt I was swimming in a very beautiful bath, and drinking mouthfuls of water, when a shower of grape-shot started us to our feet. A foolish artilleryman had lighted a port-fire close to us, and, thanks to his stupidity, the enemy opened fire on us in a moment.

At daylight the word of command came, 'Fall in; quick march,' and we advanced in the direction of the enemy's works, for they had entrenched their camp. A rush and a wild hand-to-hand fight ensued, bayonets *versus* Sikh swords. One man had his four fingers cut clean off against the barrel of his musket as he drove the bayonet home.

In a very short time, we had possession of the camp, and the first thing I did was to seize a bucket standing at the muzzle of a gun (the water black as ink) and pour it down my throat. For a moment I felt nothing, and then an acute pain attacked me, as if I had swallowed a sword, caused by my not having had a drop of water for twenty-four hours. The enemy went clear away, and we did not attempt to follow them beyond their camp, where the tents were left standing.

We discovered a well. I got a bucket, and made a long line for it by cutting off a lot of ropes from the tents and tying them together. There was such a rush to the well that I was nearly pushed in, and had to get a party of men to stand behind and protect me. I drew the water as fast as possible, while the mob standing round almost fought for it, and during the time I was at work, Sir Hugh Gough came up with one or two of his staff, and it was some time before he got any water, as there was nothing to drink out of but my bucket; the men were too mad with thirst to pass it even to the commander-in-chief.

My little party then went foraging for something to eat, and came upon a quantity of fine oranges in a tent. After a great feast, we thought of the other men of the company. Mine, by the way, was No. 1 of the first brigade of the first division of the Army of the Sutlej. How were we to carry the oranges? A bright idea struck us. We pulled off a dead man's trousers, tied up the end of the legs, and carried off our prize. I made the pay-sergeant fall in the company and gave every man two oranges. However, before they were devoured an alarm was given that the enemy's cavalry were coming, and the regiment rapidly formed square, and then occurred an incident that I can vouch for.

The governor-general, Lord Hardinge, with his son and one native trooper, rode into our square. It appeared afterwards that he had sent his escort back with the Crown Prince of Prussia (whose doctor, his only attendant, had been killed that day), and the prince went right away out of India, but I really don't know by what route he went. The governor-general addressed us in a firm voice: 'Thirty-First, I was with you when you saved the Battle of Albuera; behave like men now.' He then took the star off his breast and gave it to his son. He evidently never expected to leave our square alive, and up to that time we had no idea that anything was wrong, but in some unaccountable way the greater part of our army had melted away in the night, and Sir Harry Smith's division was left almost alone to face a fresh army, the formed line of which we could see advancing upon us in perfect order, and as this was a war where no quarter was asked or given on either side, and we had to fight it out to the bitter end, things looked very black indeed. We had not a gun left, or if there were, the ammunition was all expended; but most of them were smashed; and dead horses and broken limbers were lying about, having been completely outmatched by the heavier artillery of the Sikhs.

The fresh army halted a good way off and opened fire, and this went on for hours, the enemy evidently thinking that our army was in the empty Sikh camp, and that we had set a trap for them. I fell fast asleep, and awoke with a start to find the men on their feet, and wildly pointing to our left front we saw the 3rd Light Dragoons and a regiment of native cavalry riding straight for the enemy's flank, a mere handful of men attacking 10,000. We cheered wildly, and fancy our rage when, just as the dragoons closed with the enemy, our native cavalry turned tail and bolted. We gave them a volley as they disappeared in the dust, and before it and the smoke cleared away not a man was to be seen; the whole Sikh Army had bolted! I always believed, and I still do, that the Sikh general had received an enormous bribe to retire; for while we were still wondering, Sir Harry Smith rode up to us and said, 'I congratulate you, 31st; there's not an enemy within ten miles.' Thus, ended the memorable two days' fighting at Ferozesha.

Here is a newspaper extract which I still have:

The 31st, this gallant old corps, seems to have received more than its share of hard knocks in the four last glorious battles it was engaged in. At Ferozesha it was merely the cool and determined fighting of this regiment and the old 50th that saved Sir H. Smith's division from destruction, as they found themselves in the midst of the Sikh camp quite unsupported.

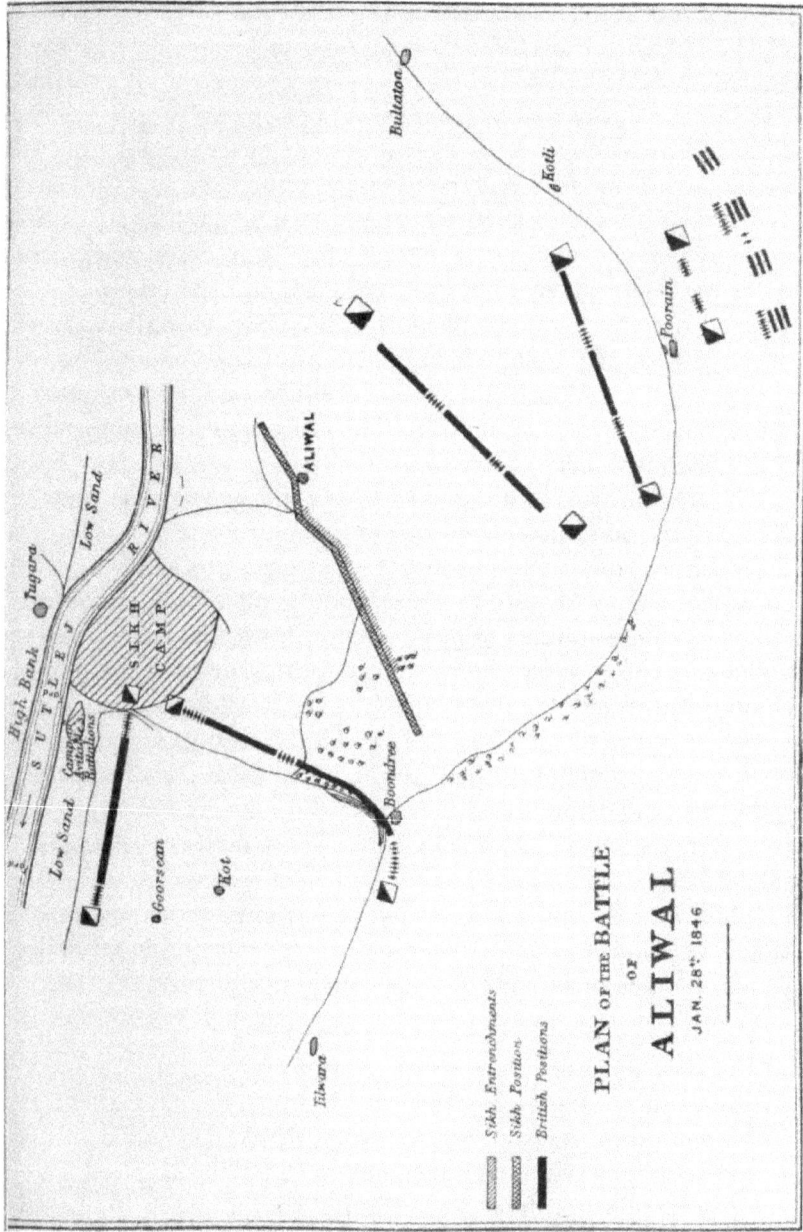

PLAN OF THE BATTLE
OF
ALIWAL

JAN. 28TH 1846

	Sikh Entrenchments
	Sikh Position
	British Positions

Bultatoa.

Kotli

Pooraan.

ALIWAL

SIKH RIVER

High Bank Tugara

Low Sand

Low Sand

SUTLEJ

Low Sand

SIKH
CAMP

British
Battalions

Goorsean

Kot.

Boondree

Tibwad

The 50th were certainly there also, but so were the 29th, and I am certain it was with them that we formed line as I have stated above.

After the fight we took possession again of the Sikh camp, and remained there another day, while the army was being got into shape again. Quite a number of men had gone off during the night, a report having been spread that the army were to retire upon Ferozepoor, and in the dark they had actually passed this second Sikh Army, which came down upon us the next morning. It was at the beginning of the fight that poor Pollard was killed he who saved my life at Moodkee. The adjutant was also killed, and from that day I had to take his place.

The doctor of the Crown Prince of Prussia was also killed in the earlier part of this engagement, and Lord Hardinge sent the prince from the field with his own escort (as I have already related), which accounts for his entering our square with only one man and his son. On the crown prince arriving at home he expressed his wish to the British Government that he might be allowed to present the decoration of the Iron Cross to the officers with whom he had fought in these battles, and I was told that the reply was that officers of the British Army were not allowed to wear foreign decorations. I have always felt that being deprived of this decoration was a deep and lasting grievance, and I think the German emperor should send us it yet—at least, to the few survivors of these memorable battles.

After this I had to command my company as well as fulfil the adjutant's duties, and act as postmaster, which was a most troublesome berth, as in those days all letters had to be paid for on delivery, as well as sorted, being sent up in sacks. I had to get them delivered and collect the pay.

As the commissariat had not arrived, we had just to forage for ourselves. I got hold of a bag of native fine flour, a lot of *ghee* (clarified butter), and a big brass basin, which I polished well with sand; then lighted a fire, boiled the water, and made a fine dish of porridge, making a wooden spoon out of a bit of stick. Just as I was having a feast the colonel came up, and I offered him some; but, being an Englishman, he could not be persuaded to try it. I enjoyed the foraging very much; it was certainly not plundering, and I may just relate another little incident: I saw one of my men with an axe in his hand, and asked him what he wanted with that. 'Look here, sir,' he said, and taking me into a grand-looking tent, showed me the tent-pole plated with silver in the most beautiful patterns.

We cut it right down one side with the axe. It was very thick, and that ancient tent-pole would have been a prize for the British Museum. Having chopped it (the silver) in two halves, and knocked it into two flat bundles, we had each as much solid silver as we could carry. I put my share inside my military cloak, which I had strapped on my back; but the very first day's march I was so tired of my load that I threw it into a ditch. We marched in the direction of the Sutlej and encamped on the banks of the river. The main body of the army was now encamped not very far above Ferozepoor, and we heard that the enemy had constructed a bridge of boats and were fortifying a large camp on British territory.

Word also came that an army of Sikhs had crossed the river near Ludhiana and were threatening our rear and communications. Sir Harry Smith was dispatched at once, and the 31st, of course, was one of his regiments.

After several days' march back towards Umballa, Sir Harry got word that the enemy were encamped between us and Ludhiana. We marched all night to attack them, and as we marched, some of their spies set fire to the bushes some little distance on our right flank, repeating this from time to time, so that the enemy knew exactly where we were. We found them in possession of a large walled city, with a battery of guns drawn up in front of the principal gate on an eminence.

From there, as soon as we came within range, they opened a heavy and most destructive fire on us.

We were marching in column of companies, their fire taking us at an angle. One shot which I saw killed seven men. Lieutenant Timbrell was commanding the company in front of me, with a soda-water bottle of cold tea resting on his hip. A round shot cut the bottle from his hip without touching him, and even without his knowledge; and when I came up to it, I picked it up, emptying it of its contents.

After some manoeuvring we formed line and advanced against the enemy. Sir Harry Smith was looking at them through his glass, and I heard him remark distinctly, 'It won't do today; they are too strong for us.'

We then changed our direction and marched for Ludhiana, and as long as we were within range of their guns they kept up a heavy fire upon the column, and we lost more men that day than in the Battle of Aliwal (fought a few days later, January 28, 1846), this being the Battle of Budiwal, fought on 21st. Both men and horses were terribly knocked up, and the infantry had to help to drag the guns, many of

THE 3RD KING'S LIGHT DRAGOONS IN THE FIRST SIKH WAR

the officers doing their share. It is a great mistake, in my opinion, to fight a battle after a long march, and on this occasion we found it to be so, as the enemy were in a fortified town, with a high solid brick wall all round, and had we charged the guns outside the gate, we should have been helplessly shot down from the walls. Sir Harry's information must have been very bad, or he would never have attempted to attack the enemy in such a position. The first water we came to was a pool of mud in which the cattle had wallowed for a long time, and it was almost as thick as soup, and very filthy. But we rushed in up to our knees and drank greedily, scooping up the mud with our hands. Most of the men, myself among the number, were very ill after it, and we suffered many other hardships that are never recorded in the grand accounts of battles that appear in history.

As soon as the firing commenced, our long train of baggage and the camp-followers and sick men, who were being carried in *doolies*, were deflected out of range of the enemy's shot, and circled round through the jungle, in the direction of Ludhiana; and when we retired from the fight, the enemy, seeing the baggage unprotected, rushed out upon it, killed everyone they could get hold of, indiscriminately, and plundered everything. Scarcely any of our camp-followers were killed; they took to their heels like greyhounds. The two *syces* who were leading my horses jumped on their backs and galloped hard, arriving at Ludhiana long before we did. I lost everything but the clothes I stood up in, and the post-bag with the undelivered letters, and for months afterwards I was worried by the postmaster-general to send him the postage. I referred him to the enemy who had looted the post-bag.

A good many other officers were as badly off as myself; but as the baggage had scattered, some of it found its way safe to Ludhiana, and Timbrell's tent arrived all right; so I had at least a covering over my head, though I had to sleep in my clothes on the ground. The Indian Government was remarkably good and liberal under the circumstances, as we got handsome remuneration for everything that was lost. Four of us were provided with a soldier's tent, and there was no difficulty in Ludhiana in getting *charpoys* and a supply of Indian quilts and sundry other necessaries, so we soon made ourselves as comfortable as circumstances would permit.

After two or three days we returned to Budiwal, as the Sikhs had retired to the banks of the Sutlej, and we found our poor sick men lying killed in the jungle, most of them in the *doolies*, as they had been shot as they lay in bed by the muzzle of a musket being put against their side. You can imagine how savage the men were after such a sight.

Little Tritton lost everything, like myself, so he and I adjourned by ourselves to a house, stripped, and washed our shirts, then set the house on fire, held up our shirts till they dried, put them on, and went quietly back to the regiment.

At the place our baggage had been plundered, letters and papers were lying about all over the ground, and many of the letters were picked up and read, I am ashamed to say. I remember being much amused at hearing one read out from people that we did not know. It was from a wife in England, giving her husband instructions how to curry favour with someone in power, and thereby get a good fat staff appointment!

We carefully interred all our poor murdered comrades and returned to Ludhiana.

Our next movement was to follow the enemy to Aliwal. Close to the town of that name they had established a camp on the banks of the Sutlej.

We marched early in the morning, and after passing over some rising ground, we descended to the level of the river on to a magnificent flat plain, extending for miles in the direction of the enemy's entrenched camp. Sir Harry Smith formed his forces in order of battle, the infantry in line, with the artillery at intervals, and the cavalry on the flanks. We marched steadily forward.

Our grenadier company was on the extreme right of the line, and I came next with No. 1 Company of the 31st.

Soon the enemy opened fire at long range, and at first the shot failed to reach us; but we soon had it come hopping along like cricket-balls, and we could distinctly watch it coming.

They passed either through or over the line; but soon a shell burst right in front of my company, and several of the men fired at it.

I was blowing up my right-hand man for being so foolish, when a round shot cut half his cap from his head without hurting him. It smashed the arm of Mitchell, the man immediately behind him, and cut off the haversack of a third man, in which he had a loaf of bread. This went rolling away to the rear; he immediately ran after it and picked it up amidst a good deal of chaff from his comrades. As we got close up to the enemy, I saw that there were two guns directly in front of us, and my men peppered the gunners so effectually as to speedily reduce their numbers to two.

Just then a mounted man rode right at us all alone, and I ran out to meet him; but before we met both he and the horse rolled over dead, shot by my own men behind. He fell right at my feet, and I picked up his sword. At that moment I distinctly saw one of the two gunners who were left put a charge of canister-shot into the gun, and then his comrade fired right in our faces. I instinctively put my arm across my eyes, and got a shower of dust and sand in my face, while the sole of one of my boots was ripped off right to the heel, but I myself was totally unhurt.

My company then made a rush at the guns. Another charge of canister was put down by the same man, while his comrade stood ready with the port-fire, when just at that moment he was shot dead, falling down on the light. His companion, seeing him fall, ran to pick up the port-fire; but it was extinguished. He immediately turned round upon us, drew his sword, and rushed forward, waving it above his head, and died in front of his guns. Such were the brave men with whom we had to contend. I was first up to the guns, and marked the howitzer by a sharp stroke of the Sikh's sword, which I had picked up shortly before, across the muzzle, making a notch thereby, while one of the men wrote with a piece of chalk "31" on the guns.

I took the linchpin out of the wheel of the other gun (it was a lion's head in brass), and put it in my pocket. These two guns were bronze, and highly ornamented and beautifully inlaid on the carriages, and, I believe, had been a present from some former governor-general to Runjeet Singh.

Two days afterwards, when I heard that the guns were to be sent home to the queen at Windsor, I went quietly back and replaced the linchpin with its lion's head in its place.

The fight now became general, and I saw a magnificent charge of the 16th Lancers, who rode right through one of the enemy's squares. As they, the lancers, came round our right flank, and galloped in front of the infantry line, a regiment of *sepoys*, our own men, opened fire upon them, and I rushed down the front of their line, knocking up the muskets with my sword, and shouting in Hindustani, 'Our men, our own men!' It was a great wonder I was not shot, for some of the muskets were fired right in my face; but men can do wonderful things and escape in the heat of battle.

Referring to the guns that we took that day, I believe they were planted in front of some part of Windsor Castle, but I have never seen them. I wonder if the notch I made with my sword is still to be seen on the muzzle of the howitzer.

After some rather hard fighting we drove the enemy right across the Sutlej, and took possession of their camp.

The battle was scarcely over when a prisoner was brought up to the colonel, in charge of a corporal and two men. He turned out to be an Englishman who had deserted from the Bengal Artillery many years before and joined Runjeet Singh's Army, in which were both English and French officers, for Runjeet was very fond of getting them to assist him in that grand army he was so proud of. This man had the rank of colonel, and I at once recognised him as the officer who was with the guns that gave us such a mauling at Budiwal, and I told him that I saw him there, but he stoutly denied it. Here the corporal, saluting the colonel, said in his Irish brogue: 'There's a *nullah* quite handy; shall I take him down there?' at the same time significantly tapping his musket. 'No,' said the colonel, 'you scoundrel; take him to the main guard!' This man was ultimately pardoned by the authorities, but I know not what became of him afterwards.

We then returned to the main army, and found that Sir Hugh Gough was waiting for us to make a grand attack on the enemy's camp at Sobraon, which was strongly entrenched.

CHAPTER 6

The Battle of Sobraon

On the morning of February 10, 1846, the whole army advanced towards Sobraon.

The first division, in which we were, was on the right flank, and we were destined to attack the enemy's camp close to the Sutlej.

The camp may be described as roughly a half-circle, resting on the River Sutlej. It was protected all round by a rampart 9 or 10 feet high, with portholes constructed of wood, on a level with the ground outside, which could, therefore, be swept with grape-shot. The bridge of boats was about half-way from the two corners of the camp, so you may judge what a desperate undertaking we had before us. We were just halted out of range, and a little to our left were the 9th Lancers. The enemy occasionally sent a long shot over their heads, and I remember distinctly watching how every man slightly bowed his head in his saddle as the shot whistled past, and all the pennons of the lances moved forward and then back again in the most perfect unison; for when a round shot is coming in one's direction, as the sound rapidly increases in volume, it is almost impossible to resist the idea that the shot is going to strike yourself.

After a short, far too short, bombardment, which has been severely criticised since (as it resulted in a terrible loss of life to our army, and left the enemy quite unshaken), the whole force advanced to the attack. We found ourselves in front of a tremendous rampart, 10 or 12 feet high, with portholes for guns, built with wood near the level of the ground, while the top of the rampart was held by men with only the head and shoulders visible. They kept up a terrific fire on us, for the men were all picked shots, and as fast as a man fired, he handed his musket to the men behind him, when a loaded one was handed back in return. Three times we got close up to the works, and three times we were driven back. During these attacks both the officers carrying the colours were mortally wounded—Ensigns Tritton and Jones. The latter died at once.

My poor little subaltern, Tritton, just before we were ordered to advance under fire, had come to me for a drink of cold tea, and while he was opening the flask the order came, 'Fall in!' 'Ah!' he said, 'it's always the way; when I want a thing, I can't get it. Never mind, I'll have some by-and-by.' These were the last words he spoke to me.

After the two officers carrying the colours fell, Corporal McCabe picked up the regimental colour, rushed forward, climbed the embankment, and planted it there. How he escaped being riddled with bullets was simply miraculous, and with a loud cheer the whole brigade rushed forward and established themselves inside the enemy's camp, then, after some desperate fighting, they forced the enemy to retire across their bridge of boats. I actually saw them marching (not running) with their arms sloped in a most defiant manner, but when they got on to their bridge of boats, it gave way, and our artillery at once opened fire on them, making fearful havoc, while the river swept them away in hundreds. My subaltern, little Tritton, although shot right through the head, lived till night. I knelt beside him, holding his hand in mine till he expired. Poor boy! I cut off a lock of his hair and gave it into his mother's hands when we were quartered at Walmer. She lived at Canterbury, and when I took the hair out of the same paper in which I had first folded it, some sand from the battlefield where he fell dropped out. We gave him a soldier's grave, as we were under orders to march again in the morning, and every available *doolie* was required for the wounded.

It was a very miserable night for those that were left, and I am not ashamed to say my eyes were wet as I knelt by my dear comrade's bedside in the dreary, dark tent—a soldier's tent in which four of us were quartered after we lost all our baggage at Budiwal; and here was I left all alone, the other three killed or wounded.

But to return to the battle. Our Horse Artillery had got into the camp by an opening close to the river, and had thus been able to open fire upon the bridge of boats at short range, and it was this battery, I believe, that smashed the bridge. Captain Garvock, who was on Sir Harry Smith's staff, was hit on the leg by a ball that passed through the flesh without touching the bone; as he could feel it under the skin on the other side, he coolly took out his penknife and cut it out there and then, and stuck to his duty till the battle was over! Lieutenant Law had

THE BATTLE OF SOBRAON, 10TH FEBRUARY, 1846

a ball stuck in his shoulder-blade, and he refused to have it cut out, and I fancy it never *was* taken out, as it was there years after. Timbrell, my chum, had a terrible smash; a heavy iron grape-shot passed through both thighs, smashing both bones, and lodging under the skin like Garvock's on the far side. Sergeant Meredith carried him out of action back to back, and Timbrell told me what a fright he got when, looking down, he saw his two heels where his toes ought to have been; both his legs had turned right round.

The doctor told me he was mortally wounded, and I went to see him as soon as possible. Imagine my surprise to see him sitting up in bed with a cheroot in his mouth; they said it was nothing but sheer pluck kept him alive. For many months he was kept with both his legs resting in a kind of box, the feet being fixed in their correct position at the far end; in this way both legs remained the same length. Had the feet not been fixed, one leg would have been longer than the other. As it was, his height was reduced nearly 4 inches. He afterwards rejoined the regiment, and was my subaltern when quartered at Maryborough in 1849.

An amusing incident in connection with this battle occurred some years afterwards on the pier at Kingstown, near Dublin, where all the beauty and fashion were promenading to hear the band play. A captain, formerly of the 50th Regiment, who was then living on his pension, suddenly rushed up to me, threw his arms round my neck, and shouted at the top of his voice: 'He saved my life! he saved my life!' At this everybody crowded round, and then the captain, turning about to his audience, said with the tears in his eyes: 'When I was lying desperately wounded at the Battle of Sobraon, and begging for a drop of water, he'—pointing to me—'took off a dead man's shoe, ran down to the river and brought me a drink.' This was quite true, as I filled the shoe three times for him.

Having thrown a fresh bridge of boats across the Sutlej, the whole army crossed over into the Punjab, and commenced the advance upon Lahore, the capital city. It was a grand sight to see us marching in order of battle, one long line of infantry sweeping forward with our artillery, and supported by the cavalry; but no enemy appeared to dispute the advance. The first morning a frightened stag galloped along the front of our line, and just as he had passed in front of the 31st, a Ghoorka sergeant stepped out some paces to the front, knelt down on one knee and fired, and the stag rolled over at once a beautiful shot. In due time we arrived at Lahore, and encamped just outside the city. The son of our old major (who had by this time left the regiment, Major Van Courtland) came to see us. He was a colonel in the Sikh Army, but had remained at Lahore and had not been fighting against us. I and two or three of the other officers went a ride with him, and he conducted us all through the city, and wound up our ride by taking us on to the top of one of the city gates, where we were most kindly received by the guard, who even waited upon us while we drank champagne. We were told afterwards that we had run a great risk, but all ended well. It must be remembered that at this time peace had not yet been signed.

A few days after, a grand *durbar* was to be held, to arrange the terms of peace. I was in command of the guard of honour, and saw everything most comfortably. An immense tent was pitched, in which the governor-general with the commander-in-chief and staff received all the great Sikh princes and chiefs. They arrived on elephants, gorgeously draped, and as they walked past me into the tent, I had a good look at them. They appeared to be very anxious and uneasy, evidently suspecting treachery, and under their grand draperies I could see that they all had coats of chain armour. I presented arms as they walked past, and the last to go in was Duleep Singh, so well-known for many years in this country. He was then quite a small boy, being carried in his bearer's arms, and at the entrance the bearer took off the little prince's slippers and left them at the door.

They were beautiful works of art, and embroidered in gold. I took one up and put it in my pocket, but thought that it might be considered an insult, so placed it quietly back again. I stood at the door of the tent, but could not hear what was said, and saw grand presents being presented and exchanged. When the chiefs came out, I presented arms again, and they hurried to their elephants just as a salute was being fired in their honour from a battery of siege guns, which made a terrible row and smoke.

One day Noel and I were wandering about, and came upon some of our men, who appeared to be looting from a beautiful old mosque, while a native was shouting lustily, when Sir Harry Smith rode up, and, without asking any questions, laid into the men with a cane he had in his hand. The men ran away back into camp, laughing and evidently thinking it a good joke to be thrashed by a general! We went inside and saw that the dome of the roof was highly ornamented with beautiful encaustic tiles, and almost at the highest part of the dome there was a hole right through, as if a shell had dropped in. We got

74

The 3rd Light Dragoons at Sobraon

upon the roof, I really don't remember how, as we wanted some of the tiles, and I offered to try and reach them if Noel would hold my feet. I actually got in head and shoulders through the shot-hole and dug out a lot of tiles, but to get back again was the difficulty. There I was, hanging by my heels head down, with the prospect of a 60-feet drop on to the pavement below.

After a desperate struggle, and clinging on to the sides of the hole with my nails, and Noel pulling his best, I got back again. Some of these tiles are now in the Museum of Science and Art in Edinburgh, with several other things which I presented, among them my ancestors of Inchbrakie's old charter-chest.

On our return to camp with the tiles I found a note waiting for me, saying Captain Lugard wanted to see me. He was at headquarters (on account of the tremendous casualties among the general staff), acting as adjutant-general and Sir Hugh Gough's right-hand man, although only a captain in the 31st Regiment. He told me that the governor-general had decided to send home a large party of wounded men to England, as a proof that the war was over, and informed me (a young subaltern) that I might have the command. He also said that the regiment was to go home at once *via* Calcutta, but that I should be home six months before them. Of course, I joyfully accepted the offer.

'You must leave tomorrow morning for Ferozepoor, and I will send a cavalry escort with you, as a large part of the Sikh Army are still wandering about.'

'All right,' I said, 'I am ready, and very many thanks for your kind remembrance of your old subaltern.'

The next morning about three an escort appeared, and I, with my dispatches in my cap (having nowhere else to put them) from the commander-in-chief to the general commanding at Ferozepoor, set off on the long ride, my orders being that they were to be delivered that day. I was dressed in a scarlet jacket and black trousers, and had my sword on. My baggage was to follow. I, however, took my second horse, and away I started with an escort of fifty men and an officer. About midday we arrived at a camp that had been established to keep open our communications; there the officer commanding my escort announced that his horses were done up and that he could go no further till next day.

I replied, 'My orders are to go to Ferozepoor today, and I'll go whether you come or not.'

The officers in the camp did their utmost to persuade me not to go, saying that there was no road through the jungle (which was quite true), and that they had no guide to give me. However, after a good lunch, I started alone on my second horse, trusting to my bump of locality to find my way through the jungle. Most fortunately, just after starting, I met a strong detachment, escorting a battery of heavy guns. I asked them where they came from, and they said the bridge of boats. My next question was, 'Do you think your gun-wheels have left a mark through the jungle?' and they said, 'Yes.' However, as it turned out, every now and then the marks had become invisible, and I had to cast forward until I found them again. Sometime after, I came to a sort of road with a fence on each side, evidently leading to a village. I followed the road and suddenly found myself in an open space, and rode right into the middle of a regiment of the enemy!

Some were drawing water, and many were standing or sitting about, evidently halting for their midday rest. I was going at an easy canter at the time, and without either slackening or quickening my pace I cantered right through the middle of them. My only fear was that I should ride against some of them, as they were thickly scattered about. My scarlet jacket immediately attracted their attention, but they simply stared at me in astonishment, and I smiled and nodded at them amiably as I rode past. Not a man raised his hand against me, but when I had passed the last of them, I had a most uncomfortable feeling, expecting every moment to get a shot in the back. However, nothing happened, and as long as I was in sight, I kept up the same easy pace. Then I went off pretty hard until I got some miles between me and my friends.

Without further adventure, and just about sundown, I arrived at the bridge of boats. There I found an old friend, Harry Yule (afterwards Sir Harry Yule). He had lived in the same terrace in Edinburgh as I did when we were boys together. He was most hospitable—fed my horse, gave me a good tea, and provided a guide to take me to Ferozepoor, which, he informed me, was at least ten miles off. He was in the Bengal Engineers, and then in charge of the bridge of boats. He afterwards rose to distinction in India.

It was quite dark before we started, and I could only see the white figure of the guide in front of me as he trotted along, taking a bee-line across country with a great many low mud fences to cross. The manner in which my mount kept his feet, as he scrambled over these impediments, was quite wonderful. He was a Kabul horse which the regiment had brought back with them, and was the most sure-footed animal I had ever ridden. At last, about ten o'clock at night, we came in sight of the lights of the town, and, most providentially, at the very first door I rode up to I found a party of our own wounded officers with Dr. Stewart in charge.

Of course, they were greatly surprised at my sudden appearance. They were playing cards, and looked as if they had seen a ghost when I entered. There sat poor Law with a bullet in his shoulder-blade (which he would never allow to be removed); Pilkington with smashed ankles; Flasket with his twisted and smashed foot—all brother officers of the 31st.

Dr. Stewart at once ordered a bed to be put up for me in his own room in the hospital, which was close by. I was quite stupefied with fatigue, and had scarcely thrown myself on my bed when Dr. Stewart rushed in from the surgery exclaiming, 'I'm a dead man! I'm a dead man! I have swallowed a fearful overdose of laudanum!' The hospital sergeant followed him in with two orderlies, who seized him and began to rattle him up and down the room, saying, 'This is your only chance, sir; this is your only chance.'

Poor man! he only groaned out, 'Oh, let me lie down!' I shall never forget the horrors of that night. They dragged him up and down, and every now and then threw him on my bed. I was past sleeping altogether, and lay awake staring at them, as they hustled and knocked him about. Towards daylight the sergeant thought that the worst was over; they then let him lie down, and he recovered all right.

To add to the horrors of that night, there was only a door between us and the wounded men, which stood open. Some of them were moaning in agony, while others were cursing at the disturbance keeping them awake all night.

It was altogether very horrible to me in my exhausted condition, after a continuous ride from 3 a.m. until 10 p.m.

Next morning I presented my official documents to the general, and matters were put in train. Two hundred men were to be selected out of the different hospitals, and were of all arms of the Service— Cavalry, Infantry, and Artillery.

All the doctors did was to select the men. I had to find out from themselves rank, name, and all particulars, and to make a correct list myself. I had, for instance, to go into a ward and ask, 'Any men here for England?' and I might get a joyful answer, 'Yes, I am,' or a groan, 'Oh, I shall never see England again!' When the boats were ready the embarkation commenced, and two doctors were put in charge—Dr.

Rutherford and Dr. Laing. I got on splendidly with them, and during the whole nine months we were together not a disagreeable word passed between us, to the very best of my recollection. Dr. Rutherford rose to the highest post as an Inspector-General of Hospitals. Doctors were not created majors and colonels in my day. Dr. Laing was ordered back to India, while we were quartered at Walmer, in Kent, and I went off in a small boat and boarded the ill-fated *Birkenhead* in the Downs, and was the last of his friends to say goodbye to him. The terrible shipwreck on the south coast of Africa, in which his life was lost, is a matter of history.

Before sailing from Ferozepoor Lieutenant Paul arrived as an escort with forty men of the 31st, and I proceeded to arrange our fleet of fifty boats. A temporary house had been constructed on each boat of bamboos and straw, the boats being very much like a Thames barge—quite flat, with a 3-foot gunwale all round. I handed over one boat for the doctors, took one for myself, and selected a guard-boat, in which were placed one sergeant and ten men, and their only duty was to take charge of the treasure-chest, in which were put *rupees* for the men's pay, also all my own valuables—the Sikh sword and the Kytul dagger, the tiles, and sundry other things, letters, etc. Had they not been in the guard-tent I should have lost all in the fire of which you will hear presently. We had also commissariat and cooking boats, and in the rest of the fleet the doctors arranged the wounded men as they thought best, with one or two of the escort in each to act as hospital orderlies.

Our order of sailing was the same every day. The doctors' boat went first and kept in front. When they halted for the night the other boats made fast to the bank below them, one by one as they arrived. I came last and passed everything before mooring. By this arrangement the doctors began their visits the moment they arrived, and worked their way down to the lowest boat, which prevented any delay. I was very much cheered as I rode up to the boats the first day from Ferozepoor by hearing a hearty voice call out, 'Oh, boys, it is our own little officer that is to command us!' This was Mitchell, of my own company, who had lost his arm at Aliwal by the same shot that knocked half of my right-hand man's cap off.

For a few days we had a native cavalry escort, but they soon left us. From the Sutlej we sailed into the Indus, where the banks on our side were covered with jungle and almost uninhabited. I had my faithful dog Chuffy, whom I had had for years, and he followed me everywhere. He saved my life at the expense of his own. For as I returned after dark one night from the doctors' boat to my own, while making my way through the jungle along the bank of the river, I heard a slight squeak behind me, and Chuffy was gone in a moment, without another sound! Had he been in front of me the tiger would have taken me instead of Chuffy.

After that I took no more night walks, but a few days after some of the enemy, or, at all events, an enemy, brought down a gun to the opposite side of the river, and commenced to practise at our boats. The only thing that we could do was to extinguish all the lights and stay as quiet as possible until morning; but shortly before daylight, when everyone was fast asleep, they came over in a boat, crept stealthily up the bank of the river, and my boat being the first thing they reached, they threw some burning charcoal on to the thatch and made off. I awoke to a blazing fire, and dashed into the bathroom, where there was a row of large *chatties* filled with water for the morning bath, and threw the water with all my might against the flames.

Of course, it only returned on myself, as the fire was overhead, and I immediately recognised that the thing was hopeless; so, I made for the door, which was fastened, and while I was struggling to open it, a dense cloud of smoke rolled down upon me. In another moment I should have been insensible from suffocation, but with a tremendous effort I tore the door open, and after gasping for breath in the fresh air, made my way on shore along a plank. The servants also, who were sleeping in front of the boat, escaped, and at break of day there I stood, shivering in a wet shirt and nothing else, watching the boat burn to the water's edge and sink.

There I was, eleven days from the nearest station where I might get clothing of any kind, and nobody had much to lend me. However, I borrowed a suit of clothing and a pair of slippers, with a couple of towels for a *pugaree*, and took possession of a very small boat which contained commissariat stores and comforts for the sick men. At the first station we came to, the name of which I forget (it was either Succar or Roree Bukar), I was hospitably entertained by some of the officers, and succeeded in getting some decent clothing.

When arriving at a military station, it is etiquette to report your arrival to the general in command, and my experience of the ceremony was invariably the same:

The general is seated in his chair; I am introduced, and, making a polite bow, I remark, 'I am come to report the arrival of the wounded men from the Sutlej.'

The general then looks up with a severe expression on his face, and remarks, 'And pray, young man, why doesn't the commanding officer come and report for himself?'

I meekly reply, 'Please, sir, *I* am the commanding officer.'

The general then looks me up and down again, and after apologising for his mistake, asks me to be seated. I was only a youth, and looked even younger than I was. At Succar we exchanged our river-boats for small flat-bottomed steamers, used for navigating the Indus. These took us right out to sea from the mouth of the river, where two large men-of-war steamers were waiting to ship us to Bombay.

The transference was a very troublesome affair, as the flat-bottomed steamers rolled fearfully, but at length we got the invalids all safely on board, and I followed. At the gangway my old servant, Pat Kennedy, received me, saying, 'I've got your cabin all ready, sir;' and I followed him along the deck. He opened the door, and just as I was stepping in, I was seized roughly by the collar from behind by one of the ship's officers, who exclaimed, 'Come out of that, young man; that is the commanding officer's cabin!' The same old story over again.

We arrived at Bombay without any incident worth mentioning, landed, and were quartered in empty barracks preparatory to embarking for England in 1846.

After a few weeks an East Indiaman, the *Herefordshire*, was chartered to take us home. A finer ship could not have been found for the purpose. She had a flush main-deck (with large portholes constructed for cannon, and giving magnificent ventilation in fine weather), which was the quarters of the men, both the wounded and the escort.

While the ship was everything that could be wished for, the captain, I am sorry to say, was the reverse, as you will see from what occurred on board.

Before embarkation, a committee was appointed to inspect the stores by the military authorities.

Nothing could exceed the excellence and quality of all laid before them: pork and salt beef and beautiful new biscuits, and everything else the same, and the quantity laid in was vouched for.

While this display was being exhibited on deck, there was a short passage-at-arms between the captain and the chief mate, and I caught the closing remark of the captain, who was saying with great contempt in his voice, 'Oh, he's only a boy!'—the old story over again and again. As the 'boy' had had some previous experience of the treatment of troops on board ship, he mentally resolved to keep his eyes wide open, and we had scarcely been a few days at sea, when everything of the vilest quality was served out to the troops. It subsequently appeared that all the stores and rations were of the worst possible description, and that there was nothing else on board.

I afterwards ascertained that in laying in a five months' supply for the troops, as he was compelled to do by his charter, the captain had laid in nothing whatever for the ship's company of about sixty all told. The doctors, of course, condemned the rations almost daily, and this was duly notified by myself to the captain in writing. I declined all conversation with him, but carefully kept all documents and a record of all his villainies during the voyage.

The first thing that we found out was that the buckets with which our allowance of water was measured out every morning, and which were closed at the top, only a small hole being left to prevent the water from spilling, were secretly taken down to the hold, and a false bottom put in by the cooper; this robbed us of about a quart of water from every bucket served out. But the crowning piece of villainy in the eyes of my men was that he watered the grog, and at this and the other tricks which were being played, and at the abominable food, the men became simply furious.

Of course, I protested in writing, and kept copies of all the correspondence.

One morning my acting sergeant-major came to me and reported that the men had resolved to throw the captain overboard, and that they certainly meant it. I went straight down amongst them, got the ringleaders together, and had a long talk with them, pointing out that they would ruin their own prospects and me also, that they would certainly be tried for murder as soon as we reached England, and that they would forfeit their pensions.

After a long conversation, and having exhausted all my powers of persuasion, as I was perfectly helpless to enforce obedience, they promised to leave the captain alone, on my guaranteeing that they should receive satisfaction as soon as we got home. It appeared that one of the ship's officers had crept down in the dark and had overheard our conversation, and had gone and told the captain. This put him in such a funk that he scarcely showed outside his cabin door for the rest of the passage.

After rather a long passage we anchored at St. Helena, and I went on shore and visited Napoleon's grave. On my first voyage home in 1837, I had done the same, and had taken a wander all over the little island. The grave was then undisturbed; but on this my second visit it was open, and Napoleon's remains removed to France.

I went down into the grave, and was disgusted to see that the British tourist had been there, and Smith and Jones had cut their initials on the brickwork forming the side of the grave. I brought home a cutting from the old willow hanging over his grave; this was given by a friend of mine to the Botanical Gardens in Regent's Park, and it is growing there, I believe, to the present time.

On returning on board, and while we were taking in water, I was interested to see a native alongside in a small boat catching a kind of mackerel that came about in search of food. He had only one arm, and held a short bit of string in his hand with a hook at the end; and, sitting quietly in his boat, he dexterously threw the hook over the back of a fish, and chucked it into his boat in an instant. This he did like lightning, and sometimes took them quite fast, one after the other. It is really wonderful what can be done by practice. One of the wounded men on board, who had lost the whole of one leg, used to go up the rigging as nimbly as any sailor on board, and help reef the topsails. He had been a sailor before enlisting.

But the most astonishing example of what can be done was that of an artist, who went to paint regularly in the National Gallery, London. He had no arms, not even a stump, the sleeves of his coat were slightly padded and sewn into the pockets of his jacket, and he looked just like anyone else when walking about. He copied a picture hanging next the one that I myself was engaged upon, so that we were together daily for some time. When he arrived in the morning, the attendant put up his things and laid down his paint-box, placing a sort of large cushion, like a pillow, on the ground, and left him. He sat down on this, opened his paint-box, and put out the colours with the toe of one foot, while he held the palette by his great toe with his other foot, then selected his brushes and painted away, making usually beautiful and correct copies, which were readily bought up.

He was, I believe, a Belgian, but we in the Gallery called him Mr. Tozer.

Forgive me for running away from my ship. As I stood on deck another ship sailed into the bay, the only anchorage that is to be found at St. Helena, and this only extends from point to point of the little indentation (if I may so name it) called the bay, outside which line the depth drops suddenly down to unknown limits.

Well, the ship dropped her anchor just too far out, and so, not finding bottom, she drifted away from the land under the influence of the strong trade-wind that constantly blows there from the south-west (in consequence of this direction of the wind, sailing-ships going round the Cape from home have to keep right away, nearly to South America, in coming from the north). After running out her cable to the very end she could not get it again owing to its great weight, and so signalled to us for help; and in response the second officer and some of the men were sent off in one of our boats. They got in the anchor, and then the vessel attempted to beat back into the harbour; but the wind was too strong, and after tacking backwards and forwards for three days without coming any nearer, she signalled, ' Going to Ascension,' and we had to call there and pick up our men and boat.

Ascension was in those days considered a 'man-of-war' by the British Navy, and was recorded as such in the Admiralty books. It had a captain, officers, and crew stationed there, who were treated in all respects as if they were at sea. I am really not aware if there were any other inhabitants. It is quite a small island, and dismally barren and inhospitable-looking, with a small hill, showing a little vegetation about the centre of the island. This describes it as it appeared from the sea, and we were pretty close in. Sailors used to say that it was only a cinder heap which had been swept together as useless when the world was made! No one landed, as our second officer with his boat and crew came off to us the moment the ship was sighted.

A few days after leaving Ascension we entered the Doldrums. This is a well-named portion of sea, for, as the trade-winds do not blow home, either north or south, there is a dreaded but well-known belt of calm, and through this sailing-ships have to make their way with the help of very light and variable puffs of wind which come from all directions, alternating with dead calm. We were most unfortunate, and it looked like a judgment on the mean and greedy captain, as for a whole fortnight the ship lay slowly rolling on a glassy sea, the sails, every now and again, flapping against the masts and rigging with a most weird and irritating repetition. Combined with this there was an intense burning sun right overhead and not a cloud to give us the least shadow of comfort, and to bring things to a climax, our provisions and stores, such as they were, got so low that we had to be placed on half-rations.

Many of the stores were clean expended, such as tea, sugar, and the like, and very little water left. Just picture our situation: very little to eat or drink, and that of the worst quality, the burning heat of an Equatorial sun day after day. The captain was really afraid of his life, and no wonder after what he had heard when things were going much more pleasantly. However, we got through the Doldrums at last and made straight for the Western Isles, and came to an anchor off Fayal, one of the Azores, where we were most ably and kindly assisted by Mr. Minchin, the British Consul, who invited us on shore at once, and did all in his power to find provisions, etc. He had two lovely daughters, with whom, of course, everyone fell violently in love on the spot. As for myself, I was so far gone that my poetic muse awoke, and I composed an *Ode to the Ladies*, which I will not inflict on my readers, but simply give the two first lines:

Maid of Orta, ere we part,
Give, oh! give me back my heart.'

The rest can be imagined. Orta was the little town off which we were anchored. The island of Fayal is perfectly lovely at any time, but to us, after all the miseries of our voyage, it seemed a perfect paradise! The natives came off with boatloads of lovely fruit which they parted with for a mere song to the wounded men, and the doctors encouraged them to feast upon it for the sake of their health, and it was wonderful what an improvement took place in a few days. Obstinate old wounds that would not heal closed almost at once, and another delightful thing was that, as there were no salt provisions to be procured in the island, we had to lay in a tremendous supply of fresh beef, which kept us going till we arrived in England.

Before arriving at Fayal, we lost one of the passengers, an officer, who did not die, however, of wounds, but from disease of the lungs. We buried him at sea, and as the body was committed to the deep, we fired three volleys as a token of respect. Just as the third volley went off one of the men fell flat on the deck from the recoil of his musket, and as he lay, I heard him mutter to himself, 'There go three good bullets.' His musket had not gone off during the first and second volleys, and he had loaded it three times. Having no blank cartridges on board we were obliged to use ball cartridges, hence the remark.

At length we got as far as the Downs, and the pilot having anchored till the turn of the tide, a shore-boat was hailed, and as soon as it was alongside the captain rushed out of his cabin and jumped into it. The moment he did so a shout was raised by some of the men, 'The captain's running away!' In a moment the men rushed up from below like a swarm of angry bees.

Some jumped on the bulwarks, some in the rigging, and they yelled and howled and jeered till he was out of sight.

The faces of the boatmen as this scene was being enacted were almost beyond power of description. At one moment they evidently intended to bring the captain back again, which caused a fearful addition to the howls, and I believe my men would have sunk the boat and boatmen had they come near the ship again.

We arrived safely at Gravesend without further adventures. After casting anchor, the health officer came alongside the ship and passed up a Bible in a copper cover (to protect him from infection). The chief mate, having taken possession of the Bible, had to answer truthfully all the questions put to him.

Question: 'Have you any sick on board?'

Answer: 'No; we have a shipload of wounded men, but no sickness.'

Question: 'When was your last case of illness on board?

Answer: 'At Bombay, five months ago, a sailor died of cholera.'

'Very well,' was the oracular response; 'you are in quarantine for twenty-four hours.'

If that was not tomfoolery, I do not know what was. Now for the result. One gentleman had come on board with leave, in the hopes of meeting an old friend, when up went a great yellow flag to the masthead, and he was informed that he could not go home until the next day. His lady friends had provided an entertainment at the hotel, and we could see them at the windows waving their pocket-handkerchiefs. Then, after a time, dishes were held up to signify that dinner was ready, and there he was, poor man, a prisoner till next day! But that was not the worst of the absurd regulation.

The *Herefordshire*, being an old East Indiaman, had gun-ports all along the main-deck, where the men were quartered. As soon as night closed in and all the lights were put out according to order, a lot of shore-boats slipped alongside, well provided with drink, and, as my men had no money, they proceeded to barter all their possessions for a bottle of rum or other strong drink; and the worst of it was that in the dark the men were not at all particular whose property they handed out—boots, trousers, every article of clothing went into the boats.

Soon the whole lower deck was a scene of wild intoxication, and a length of cable covered with mud improved the appearance of those who rolled on it. Even the ammunition, which had been brought up in a cask, disappeared; so, you can imagine my feelings at the horrible state of affairs which twenty-four hours of quarantine had created.

Next morning a pompous officer came on board to request that the ammunition might be handed over to him to take to Tilbury Fort.

My reply was that I had no ammunition on board, with which he was perfectly satisfied, and went away. The only thing I could do when ordered to land was to procure the whole of the omnibuses that were to be had. Into these I packed all the half-clothed men (who were more like animals than men), amidst the sympathetic remarks of a gaping crowd. 'Poor fellows, what hardship they must have gone through! They have scarcely a rag to their backs!' etc. So ended my nine months' command.

On my bringing the whole matter regarding the captain to the notice of the authorities, the case was thoroughly investigated, and the captain was heavily fined, but not so much as he deserved to be, for I am certain he made a large profit by his villainy, and, in my opinion, ought to have been much more severely punished.

As the result of the whole affair, I received from the Duke of Wellington, who was then commander-in-chief, a highly complementary letter, saying how this young officer had conducted himself to the entire satisfaction of His Grace, under most trying circumstances. I was told afterwards at the Horse Guards that the duke had very seldom, if ever, written such a letter to a subaltern, and that I ought to be very proud of it. My informant also added, 'Your name stands well here.'

I deeply regret that this letter, together with many of what I considered valuables miniatures of relatives painted on ivory, etc.—went to the bottom in the harbour of Ithaca, through the clumsiness of the Greek sailors who were landing my luggage, when my company was sent from Zante to be quartered there later on.

CHAPTER 7

Some Disagreeable Boating Experiences

As soon as all my duties connected with the detachment were finished, I got leave, which I took in Scotland, rejoining the regiment on its return from India.

Our first station was Walmer, and the Duke of Wellington (as Warden of the Cinque Ports, 1847) came to reside at Walmer Castle, and there we often met him out walking. He used to ask the senior officers—three or four at a time—to dinner; but, being then a subaltern, I had not the honour of an invitation. He reviewed the regiment on parade, and my regiment, the 31st, was the last he ever inspected. It was done more as a compliment to us than as a military duty.

He dictated one or two movements of rather an unusual character, and expressed himself highly satisfied with the way in which they were carried out. I remember very well when marching past, a party of ladies were standing close to the saluting-point, and they were criticising the officers pretty freely as they went by. I heard one lady say, 'That's the boy for me! he's always laughing'—indicating myself. Many years after, I heard the story—a rather romantic one—of that very lady. She became engaged to a young man who went out to seek his fortune in Australia; and when he was comfortably settled, he wrote for her to come out and join him. When she arrived at Melbourne, to her great dismay she discovered that he had gone off some months previously in a rush to a newly-discovered gold-diggings. To make a long story short, he was never heard of again, and there is no doubt he was murdered on the way up.

After searching and advertising in vain for months in every conceivable way, to hear tidings of the man of her heart, the lady found herself again in Melbourne with all her money gone; but being brave and good, she sat down to consider what she could do. She had written home to her friends for passage money to take her home; but in those days it took some eight months to get an answer to a letter. Having posted her letter, she went straight to a first-class hotel, told the manager her story, and offered to accept any situation. The manager and his wife at once took her in, and there she laboured patiently, looking forward to the months that would elapse before she could get a reply from home.

After she had been there some time, an old gentleman who had large business connections both there and at the Cape, having heard the lady's story, and being very much struck by her appearance, proposed to her, but was politely and firmly refused. No doubt she was still thinking of the possibility of the lost one's return.

In due time the money arrived, and she returned to England, and to the great astonishment of her family, the old gentleman from Australia appeared on the scene, proposed again, was accepted, and took her back to the Cape of Good Hope. But she never recovered from the hardships she endured, and after a time drooped and died.

Nothing very remarkable occurred at Walmer except, perhaps, a visit to a French man-of-war, the *Vauban*. She was then at anchor in the Downs, and as we were giving a ball in a few days, I was deputed to take an invitation to the French officers. Lieutenant Bray accompanied me, and we went by ourselves in a little sailing-boat that we sometimes used to hire. Coming alongside the French steamer, we were politely received, shown into the cabin, delivered our message, and got an answer to take back to the regiment. What was my disgust on coming on deck to find that the French sailors, either out of politeness or mischief—I do not pretend to know which, but probably it was the latter, as we were two officers in uniform—had rolled up the sails and taken down the mast of our boat, and were evidently awaiting the result with very gleeful faces!

As soon as we were on board, they let go the rope. As Bray was not a sailor, I told him to sit down at the helm and look quite composed. I then stepped the mast, rehoisted the sails, put the helm over, and away we went gaily to the shore. At the ball one of the French officers remarked to me: 'You all appear to be sailors as well as soldiers!'

I had a disagreeable adventure after this. Going down with a party of brother officers for our usual bathe, I saw two officers out rowing in the little boat referred to above at a long distance from the shore, but they were standing towards us. I said to the others, 'I'll go and meet them,' and so I struck out. They seemed to be aimlessly rowing about, and I had a long swim before I got near them. Then I shouted out to attract their attention, but they, mistaking the shouts for the people on shore, pulled straight back without noticing me at all. The more I hailed the more they answered back to the shore.

By this time, I realised that it was hopeless for me to attempt to swim back again, as I was quite benumbed with the cold water. All I could do was to lie on my back and gently paddle with my hands to keep my head above water, and watch the receding boat. When they arrived at the shore, the first question my companions asked was, 'Where's Robertson?' To which they replied: 'We never saw him.' Of course, they immediately turned round and pulled back as hard as they could, and ultimately picked me up, bringing me safe to shore. I need not say I did not try that game again.

Another boating experience I had occurred one warm, sultry day, with scarcely a breath of wind, when a party of us, some five or six, pulled off in a little boat to look at the far-famed Goodwin Sands. Having got as near as we cared to go, someone proposed a swim. I said: 'On one condition—that one man remains in the boat to take charge while the others are in the water.'

'All right,' said one, so we stripped and dived in. Soon a light breeze sprang up, and on my looking round at the boat, imagine my feelings on seeing that the man in charge had stripped and was swimming also, quite happy, and thinking nothing about the boat, which was sailing quietly away before a light wind. Without saying a word, I struck out after it, and several times, when I almost had my hand on the stern, away went the boat faster than I could swim.

After a fearful struggle (which was one of life or death for the whole party, you may say) I caught the boat, scrambled in, and rowed back again as hard as I could, getting back to the others not a bit too soon.

Needless to relate, I gave the one in charge a bit of my mind as to how nearly he had drowned the whole of us.

From Walmer we went to Manchester, and when marching from the railway-station to the barracks, we had a great crowd running alongside the band. An old gentleman came up close to me and looked hard into my face two or three times. Then I saw two big tears coursing down his cheeks, and suddenly he took me in his arms, gave me a great hug, and then ran away. I must have looked very foolish, for I heard the remark pretty loud, 'That'll be the prodigal come home.' I never saw nor heard of the old gentleman again.

From Manchester we were sent over to Ireland to assist in suppressing the Smith O'Brien Rebellion, and, as the barracks were all full, we were quartered in the Linen Hall, a place where in old days the linen was stored.

The officers' quarters were on the first floor, their rooms opening on to a long passage, each room having a large door (with a hasp and padlock) at one end and a barred window at the other. When the bugle sounded for parade, a mischievous young gentleman had gone down the passage and hooked up all the doors, which made us all prisoners, as the doors opened inwards. In consequence of this, I had to smash the staple of my door. To repair this damage, my servant, without my knowledge, had hammered in a big tenpenny nail.

At that time Dublin was under command of Prince George of Cambridge, afterwards the well-known Duke and Commander-in-Chief for many years. He came to see how we were situated, as he always took a deep interest in all under his command. He told the colonel that he wanted to see an officer's quarters, and the colonel, as he afterwards told me, being sure that my room would be in good order, took His Royal Highness to see it. I threw open the door, and what was my horror, as the prince came in, to see him catch his elbow on my tenpenny nail, which ripped his coat right down the sleeve! He took in the situation in a moment, and turning to the engineer officer in charge, ordered the whole of the rooms to be instantly furnished with good locks and keys, and to be informed as soon as it was done. Well done, Prince George!

Things began to look really serious in Ireland, and we were told that the would-be rebels had prepared paving-stones and bottles of vitriol on the roofs of the houses for the benefit of the soldiers as they marched through the town. Secret information was conveyed to the authorities, and we were informed that if a heavy gun was fired at nightfall it would mean that the marines and a strong detachment of sailors were to be landed from the fleet to assist us. The day passed off with perfect tranquillity, but at sunset the ominous gun was fired, and we fully expected we were in for a big row.

I and my company were trotted down to occupy the general post-office, which was so delightfully barricaded that we could neither see nor hear what was going on outside. The small door at the back was the only entrance or exit available, and not a soul had remained behind to give us any information or assistance; had we been attacked, we could not defend ourselves till the enemy had forced open the doors. We sent across to an hotel, had a good supper brought in, and made ourselves as comfortable as possible for the night; but there was no fighting, the rebellion fizzled out, and we marched back in the morning to the Linen Hall.

I was shortly afterwards sent down with my company to Maryborough, where my subaltern and I had a good time for some months, thanks to the generous hospitality of the neighbourhood, and more particularly from the kind attention of Captain Pepper, an old Peninsular officer, whose son George, strange to say, became afterwards my brother-in-law. He was then a boy at school; he afterwards joined the 31st, and served with me through the Crimea. Subsequently I was quartered at Aldershot, where I was in command of the military train. It was here that Pepper, now a colonel, fell in love with my wife's sister, Ellen Churchill, and thus became my brother-in-law.

Some years after he left the army and settled down at his own house in the neighbourhood of Salisbury, where he became a power for good, and earned the esteem of the whole district. It was when he was addressing an audience in. the market-place at Salisbury that he caught a chill, which ended fatally. I attended the funeral, and never saw anything like it or approaching to it. As the remains passed through the town on a gun-carriage, all the shops were closed, and the whole route was crowded. When we reached the cemetery, which was some distance from the town, several stirring addresses were delivered over the open grave, and it was calculated that at least 5,000 people were present on the occasion. He left behind him a widow and family of nine children, who are following in the footsteps of their noble father.

At Maryborough, in 1840, I had a very good time by engaging a native of the district, who took me to all the rivers about, and I had some very good fishing. On one occasion, when the river was very low, he instructed me in the science, of bringing home a good basket of trout. Going to a good big burn, or stream, which ran into a river, he took a bag about the size of a pillow-case, cut a stick, and, making a hoop of it, fixed the bag open. He then fitted it into the side of the burn under the bank where the stream ran strong, and going up about 50 yards with a bundle of sticks in his hand, he thrashed the water all the way down to where the bag was, making the water quite dirty, and running fast; the moment he came to the bag he pulled it out, and there, sure enough, were a lot of fine trout, that in rushing from him had gone head foremost into the bag.

There was in the neighbourhood a Mr. Scott, who showed us much kindness, and on one occasion we were invited to a ball, and to finish up with a badger hunt. Mr. Badger lived in a hole like a fox's burrow in a wood, and his habit was to feed out at night and go home to bed in the morning. Of course, the place was quite well known, so we went to the spot, and a bag with the mouth open was fixed in his hole. A good long string was attached to the mouth of the bag, just as bags are usually closed, and the end was given to Timbrell with strict orders that, as soon as the badger dived into his hole, the string was to be pulled and the badger made a prisoner. The rest of us then beat the wood in the direction of the hole, and you may imagine our disgust at finding Timbrell with a cigar in his mouth, who told us that the badger had come towards his den, but had run off again faster than he came at the smell of the cigar; so we started for home just after daylight began to show.

Our friend Brenchly (brother to the Brenchly killed at Moodkee), had a celebrated trotter with which he had won a lot of money by betting that he would ride him for a mile at the rate of ten miles an hour without breaking out of a trot, so you may suppose the rate we went towards home—we three and the groom—in his dog-cart. The groom and I were behind, Brenchly driving with Timbrell beside him. We all fell fast asleep, driver and all, when, at a sharp turn of the road, the horse went straight on, up a steep bank, and attempted to jump the wall at the top. I found myself flat on my back, and the next moment the horse's head landed on my chest. The horse had fallen clean backwards, and the cart was upside down, the shafts both snapped through, and pointing the way we had come. Brenchly and Timbrell were lying not far off, and were quite uninjured, as was the horse and myself. They pulled me out from under him with some difficulty, and then, tying the shafts with our handkerchiefs, we had to tramp home, the groom leading the horse.

From Maryborough I went up to see the new colours presented to the regiment at Dublin by Prince George of Cambridge.

The old colours, now hanging (what may be left of them) in Canterbury Cathedral, were presented to the regiment at Meerut in 1827, and I still have a small bit of each with a drop of Tritton's blood on the regimental colour. Here is an extract from *The Times* referring to the colours:

On the return of the regiment to England, new colours were

presented by His Royal Highness Prince George of Cambridge, at Dublin, in 1848. Subsequently, Lieutenant-Colonel Spence, till lately commanding, in the name of the officers, offered the old colours to the Dean and Chapter of Canterbury Cathedral, to be placed over the testimonial to the officers who fell in the Sutlej Campaign; and it having been unanimously resolved to receive them, the sculptor by order of the officers, and accompanied by Lieutenant Timbrell (who, it may be remembered, was dangerously wounded at Sobraon), in the presence of the Venerable Archdeacon Croft, the canon in residence—appointed by Mr. Austin, the surveyor to the cathedral, carefully deposited the colours, now historical records of a stirring past, solemnly but quietly, and without either pomp or parade, over the monument, so as in no way to interfere with the architecture, but to add equally to the appearance of the testimonial and nave of the cathedral.

It was on a Monday, the day following the fourth anniversary of the Battle of Sobraon, that these colours were placed immediately above the marble testimonial executed by Mr. Richardson, sculptor.

Shortly after this, Timbrell received the appointment of paymaster to a regiment at the Cape of Good Hope, and said goodbye to his old comrades in the 31st. I did not see him again till he came down to see me in the sixties at Aldershot, and, oddly enough, we went together to call upon Major Paul (the hero of the tongue), who had just returned from New Zealand. Timbrell had not seen him since the Battle of Sobraon, but it may be remembered Paul came home with me in command of the escort of the 31st on board the *Herefordshire*.

From Maryborough we marched to Athlone, where we passed two very happy years, yachting on the magnificent lake, fishing in the Shannon, and amusing ourselves generally as young men do in country quarters.

My company was the first to arrive, and we dined with the regiment we were about to relieve.

Yachting was the great amusement there, and I was immediately tackled to purchase a cutter belonging to one of the officers. They impressed upon me that there was a terrible old rogue of the name of Fagan, and that his boat, which he would no doubt wish to hire out, could always be outsailed by the *Gem*. Next morning, I had a visit from Mr. Fagan as to the hire of his yacht, the *Shamrock*. I told him what I had heard the night before as to the quality of the boats. He replied with a queer smile, 'Come, your honour, and have a sail in the *Shamrock*, and see how you like her.'

He soon found out that I was quite at home in a sailing-boat, and so he turned round and said, 'Look here, sir; my boat's the fastest on the lake, and I can beat the *Gem* easy. I'll challenge them to a race, and you shall steer. If they beat me, you buy their boat; if I beat them, you'll hire from me.'

To this bargain I consented. That night there was a tremendous scrimmage at mess, and bets were offered against Fagan in all directions, but nobody would back him.

The course was marked out, and the race came off, the *Shamrock* beating the *Gem* all to sticks, and it was a sight to see the officers' faces on the occasion. Next morning Fagan came to me in my quarters with the same quiet smile on his face, and said: 'Now, sir, I'll tell you something. By slightly shifting the ballast I put the *Shamrock* out of trim, which accounts for their always beating me; but yesterday morning I put that all right. . . . Now, sir,' continued Mr. Fagan, 'I want to ask you a favour. My eldest daughter has been waiting a long time to go to America to join some friends there, and I want you to lend me the money to pay for her passage.'

I lent him the money at once on an agreement for repayment out of the hire of his yacht. The tears came into the old man's eyes and he said, 'Sir, I may be the biggest rogue in Athlone, and nobody trusts me, but I'll stick to you through thick and thin,' and he was as good as his word. For two years he was my most devoted attendant, fishing, shooting, or yachting; we had many a day together, and we won the regatta with the little *Shamrock*, all the boats on the lake taking part.

Now I must introduce Major Baldwin. His father was an old officer who had been at the Battle of Waterloo, and was serving in the 31st when I joined the regiment, and was killed just behind me, as I have already mentioned, at the Battle of Ferozesha.

Young Baldwin got his commission to the 31st from his father having been killed in it. He appeared always to have very great difficulty in learning to swim. However, one day he was going to show me how well he could do it, and so we went out to one of the yachts that was lying at anchor in deep water. Baldwin was in the water first, and, almost before I had my clothes off, I saw him struggling with his nose under water. I jumped in at once, swam to him, and caught hold of him.

I had often heard of the danger of taking hold of a drowning man, but now I had to experience it. He instantly seized me with a grip like a vice, pinning my right arm to my side and struggling violently to get up on my shoulders. Down we went together, apparently a long way, until it appeared to be getting quite dark. I held my breath, but it was a fearful struggle to keep from gasping. Striking out hard with my feet and with my left hand, I tried to rise to the surface.

I shall never forget the horrible feeling of suffocation. I looked up as we were slowly rising, and saw the white keel of a boat overhead. By this time Baldwin had ceased to struggle, but his grip was worse than ever. With a last effort I threw up my hand. It was seized by a boatman, and I had my head above water once more. I caught the gunwale of the boat with my hand, and gasped out, 'Take *him*,' and Baldwin was dragged into the boat, and in due time revived, after which we returned to the barracks.

Imagine the time that we were under the water, when a man on shore was able to row off before we appeared above water. After this incident Baldwin and I were the best of friends.

Another great friend of his was Swaffield, and we occasionally used to play him (Baldwin) innocent practical jokes. Here is one for example:

Baldwin was out dining with the Scots Greys. His room was not far from Swaffield's, the door being down a small passage with no way through.

The fuel issued to us was peat, no coal being used in Athlone, so Swaffield and I proceeded to build a wall 4 feet high across the passage, but before that I had mischievously put a cork in his keyhole, and shaved it off smooth. We then put out the lamp in the passage, which we had scarcely done and retired to Swaffield's room, when we heard Baldwin racing upstairs, and bang he went against the turf wall. A loud shout followed, and then a rapid 'What's this? what's this? what's this?' Then he returned to the head of the stairs and shouted out for the mess sergeant: 'Sergeant Parker, bring a light.'

Parker appeared on the scene with a candle, and exclaimed: 'Dear me, sir; they have been playing a joke on you; we'll soon clear this away!' and in no time the turf was sent flying in all directions, and the sergeant said, 'There, sir, that'll,' and then retired downstairs with the light. We could hear Baldwin rummaging with his key against his door, then a series of short angry exclamations and a violent stamp on the floor. Then he hastened to the head of the stairs and shouted again for Parker. Parker once more appeared on the scene with the candle, and we heard him exclaim: 'Dear me, sir; they've put a cork in the keyhole!

'Then bring me a corkscrew,' said Baldwin.

The door was duly opened, and the poor fellow retired into it with a violent bang of his door.

By this time, we were nearly suffocated with suppressed laughter, lying on the floor with our handkerchiefs stuffed into our mouths. The next night at mess we wound up the farce. Several of the officers had got a hint that there was something funny going to happen at mess, so when I said across the table in rather a loud voice to Swaffield, 'Swaffield, I want to ask you a question,' there was a profound silence, everyone looking up, wondering what was coming next. Then I continued: 'When a man comes home from a dinner-party, and calls for a corkscrew to open his door, would you say he was drunk or sober?' Before I scarcely had the words out of my mouth, Baldwin shouted out, 'I was not drunk!' amid the laughter of the whole room.

There was an officer in the regiment who was detested by a number of his brother officers. He was generally considered what we call a 'shy bird.' He happened to be at home during the Kabul and also the Sutlej Campaigns. Now, there happened to be in Athlone at that time a little weekly newspaper called *Fiz*, and some of this officer's gentlemen friends used to show him up week by week in the paper, but after a time these articles became so spiteful that the colonel of the regiment took it up and insisted on the thing being put a stop to.

At a meeting of all the officers in the mess-room no one would acknowledge to be the author of the particular article in question, so a paper was put on the table with the following heading: 'I hereby solemnly declare as an officer and a gentleman that I did not write the article in question.'

'Now, gentlemen,' said the colonel, 'who is prepared to sign his name to that paper?'

Immediately one officer stepped forward and signed his name, followed by all the rest. I need not record the remarks the colonel made on the subject, but he evidently considered that someone had perjured himself, and the affair got talked of greatly in the town.

Two or three nights after this the editor of the *Fiz* came quietly into my room, and said to me something to the following effect: 'Things are beginning to get very hot, and I expect to be before the court about that last letter, so I have brought you all your letters back again.' And he then and there deposited a bundle on the table.

I said: 'I don't know what you mean.'

'Oh, of course you know, between ourselves; you need not say anything about it,' he said, and immediately went away.

So, I sat down and opened the packet, and what was my horror to find the original of the scandalous letter and several others that had previously appeared, together with a polite note purporting to come from myself, with my signature attached to it, the whole in the well-known handwriting of the man who was first to sign the paper at the meeting. I sat for a long time in a sort of dream. 'What am I to do?' I thought over and over again. 'If I take the papers to the colonel this officer will be irretrievably ruined, and he has a wife and family.'

The next morning, having made up mind, I called the said officer into my room with the papers on the table before me. I said to him: 'Look here, I had a visit last night from the editor of *Fiz*, and he handed over to me all the original documents,' and I held them out to him. He looked at me for a moment, and turned deathly pale. Then he staggered into a chair, and I said: 'What do you advise me to do with them?'

He gasped out: 'Burn them!' I gathered up every fragment from the table, put them together, and burned them before his eyes. No one has ever heard of this event until this writing.

I kept his secret, and I hope he was grateful. It did not strike me fully until afterwards what a position I was in myself. Had the editor been summoned before a court, he would have sworn that I was the author, that he had returned all the documents to me, that I had declared they were not in my writing, and that I had burned them. No one would have believed me; but this side of the question never occurred to me at the time.

Our regiment was very much liked in the neighbourhood, and we were constantly being entertained. At that time the art of daguerreotype had just been discovered, the forerunner to the art of photography. A married lady residing in the neighbourhood was anxious to have a second copy taken of her likeness as a surprise for her husband, who was to know nothing until it arrived. She entrusted the original to me, as I was shortly going up to Dublin.

As bad luck would have it, a brother-officer, whose room was immediately below mine in the Castle, happened to come into my room, and accidently saw the likeness, which he recognised, pounced upon it, and declared he would take it back to the husband in the morning, refusing to give it up, in spite of my demands. He rushed off with the portrait downstairs to his own room, banged the door in my face, and locked it.

I confess I was very angry. The classics say that anger is a short madness, and it certainly was so in my case. I went straight back to my room, took a brace of pistols out of a drawer, loaded one with ball, the other with powder, and took them downstairs, calling upon him to open the door.

He only jeered at me. In a moment I kicked the panel of the door to pieces, forced my way through the opening, and said to him, putting down the two pistols on the table quietly: 'One is loaded with ball, the other with powder: take your choice. We'll fire across the table at "One, two, three," and one of us won't see daylight.'

He looked at me for a moment, and then stammered out: 'It was only fun on my part.' Then he went to a drawer, took out the daguerreotype, and handed it to me. I picked it up with the pistols, and retired as I had entered. He did not send in a bill for the repairs of his door, nor did he ever refer to the transaction afterwards. I was not sorry when he left the regiment.

From Athlone we went to Enniskillen, and I passed a delightful summer on detachment, as it is called, with my own company at Ballyshannon. Loch Melvin was then celebrated for its salmon, so I engaged the services of old Pat McKay, the best fisherman in the neighbourhood, and we had a grand time of it together on the lake. By the end of the season I had landed forty salmon. I used to start very early in the morning, having my own boat and boatman on the lake, and returned late at night; the following day I devoted to military duty. In this way I fished three days a week.

From Ballyshannon we marched to Fermoy. The only incident I remember was my visit to an iron-mine on the way, and the astonishment of the miners at seeing a man in a scarlet coat and gold epaulettes down in the mine.

It was when out hunting at Fermoy that I had a terrible smash. Going with the hounds at full speed, my horse, in taking a high bank, caught his feet on the top, and turned a clean somersault into the next field. My only recollection is that, as I endeavoured to lift his head with all my might, the ground sprang up and struck me fair in the face, the horse having fallen on top of me, without my leaving the saddle. Utter unconsciousness lasted I do not know how long; but when I came to myself, I was lying on my back on the mud floor of an Irish cabin, with the occupants standing round looking at me. My mouth was wide open, packed tight full of earth, and I was choking for want of breath. I signed for water, but when they brought it in a basin, I had to dig the mud out of my mouth to enable me to breathe a little, and I felt a horrible pain in my face.

I asked for a looking-glass. They brought me a small piece which had once belonged to a mirror before it was smashed. I staggered to the window, and what was my horror to find I had no nose! it was clean smashed into my face between my eyes. I had at that moment a lively recollection of an old farrier who had had his nose kicked in flat by a horse. 'Shall I be like that man?' I thought. Immediately I went to work on the spot, and pushed and kneaded my nose back into shape, tied my pocke-thandkerchief over my left eye, which was completely shut up, mounted my horse, and rode back to the barracks. I remember the horror with which I had to jump one or two fences before I got to the high-road.

When I got to the barrack gate, I could barely see with the eye that was left open, and had to be led to my quarters. The doctor speedily came, dear old Dr. Atkinson, now also gone to join the majority. The first thing he did was to congratulate me on having re-made my own nose. 'Had you waited until you got home,' he said, 'I could have done nothing for you.' He then proceeded to oil his little finger and insert it in my nose to open the passage which was entirely closed. The operation was horribly painful. For three days I lay on my back with a lint mask on, while a hospital orderly sat by the bed night and day and kept the mask wet with a healing lotion. Being a total abstainer at the time, the rapidity of my recovery was something marvellous. Eleven days after the accident I was dancing at a ball without a mark on my face except a green tinge right across under both eyes, which was scarcely perceptible by candlelight.

I may mention some of the rows we had at the General Election shortly before this, when we were quartered at Limerick. During one of the worst the 31st had to shoot three of a band of ruffians, headed by a priest, who, armed with bludgeons and knives, attacked the voters whom the 31st were escorting to the poll. This was in 1852.

Of course, an Irish jury returned a verdict against Captain Eager and Lieutenant Hutton, and also with delightful Irish ingenuity included the colonel of the regiment, who was twenty miles away, in a verdict of wilful murder; and as we shortly afterwards embarked for the Mediterranean, these three officers had to be left behind to be tried for their lives, and it was nearly a year before we saw our colonel again.

My share in this notorious election was being sent to the town of Ennis with my company to assist in keeping the peace. We were quartered in an old distillery, and Lieutenant Prevost, who was my subaltern, took possession, with myself, of the office. I had my horse with me, stabled in a large room on the ground floor opposite the men's quarters.

As the establishment was closed by an immense gate, Tiger, the horse, was allowed to walk about in the yard sometimes, and he took to going into the room at dinner-time amongst the men. When they were at dinner, he used to walk round the table getting little tit-bits. One day one of the men, out of mischief, presented him with a hot piece of meat on the end of a fork. Tiger thought that two could play at a practical joke, so he wheeled round, lashed out, and sent the table and contents flying up in the air, fortunately without striking anyone. I heard loud shouts of laughter as I ran down to see what had happened. In future Tiger was ordered to be tied up at dinner-time.

The scenes that took place daily in the streets were beyond description. The priests at the street-corners were positively raving against the British Government and everything English. Repeal was then the order of the day, and the people were worked up into such a state of frantic excitement that they were prepared for any extravagance.

One afternoon a riot was anticipated, and I received a message from Mr. Franks, the magistrate, who was a brother of Colonel Franks, of the 10th Regiment, telling me that we were to remain accoutred and under arms all night, as a big row was expected.

It was a very still, hot summer evening, and Prevost was amusing himself with his harmonium, and, as he had a good voice, was singing. Just as he finished one of his songs, by this time well into the night, a thundering knock came to the outer gates. The sentry shouted out at the top of his voice, 'Who comes there?' and every man in the barracks jumped up and seized his arms. In a moment there was a dead silence, the men eagerly listening to know what was up. 'Who comes there?' shouted the sentry a second time, when a very small voice outside the gate replied, 'If you plaze, Mr. Sintry, will you ask the gintleman to sing that over again?' and the sentry's indignant reply was drowned in the shouts of merriment from the men.

It was about this time I was ordered to return to headquarters and be relieved by another captain. The moment the magistrates heard it they sent an urgent dispatch to Dublin Castle, without my knowledge, to say that if Captain Robertson and his men were removed from the town until after the election, they would not be answerable for the consequences. The result was that the general was ordered to leave me where I was, and so I had another fortnight of the whisky distillery.

The election presented scenes of riot beyond description. The voters who were not on the side of the priests had to be brought up in batches from the country escorted by cavalry and infantry. The poor wretches had their faces covered up with their coats, and were marched through the town amidst the yells and execrations of the people, a frantic, howling mob, hounded on by the priests. Cabbage stalks, turnips, and such-like missiles were freely hurled when they could get a shot, and I myself got a blow on the neck that nearly knocked me down, but which, of course, was intended for a voter.

When we got to the polling place things were so bad that I had to draw up my men in line to prevent the place from being stormed, and we received orders from the magistrates to load with ball cartridge. An old man came up to me and said, 'Shure, you'd never go to shoot us?' to which I replied, 'If the magistrates order me, I'll have to shoot you at once.' I heard the old man turn round to the people behind him and call out, 'Oh, boys, be aisy! The officer sez he'll have to shoot us.' This had a quieting effect, and I may mention that the priests lost the election.

After what was called 'the six-mile massacre' at Limerick, which I have before alluded to, the whole regiment were marked men. The colonel received numerous letters, some with coffins, some with skulls and cross-bones, and things got so bad at Limerick that the whole regiment had to be confined to barracks.

Shortly after this a man who had slipped out without leave came back covered with blood. In a moment a lot of his comrades seized their arms and made a rush at the gate to get into the town. The colonel and myself happened to see them, and he rushed out just as he was, without his hat, and attempted to stop them, actually hanging on by some of the men's legs as they went over the gate. The moment he saw that they had got out he turned to me and said, 'Robertson, for goodness' sake, go with them and bring them back.' That was all he said, and I was over the gate like a shot. It must be remembered that they were Irishmen too, and thoroughly roused by the many insults they had already received. They fixed bayonets and rushed down the streets. In a moment, like a flash of lightning, the street was cleared as if by magic.

Men, women, and children dashed into the nearest houses and slammed the doors. I got our men stopped as soon as possible, and said, 'Now, boys, they've done us; we'd better go back to barracks as fast as we can,' putting it in this fashion to soothe them.

They came along with me in a mob, and we found the gate open. There I said to the men, 'Be off to your rooms,' which they did at once; so, after locking the gate and taking out the key, I walked back to the mess-room, where I found the colonel very anxious. I said, 'I've got them all back again, sir, and there's no harm done. Nobody has been hurt.'

His face brightened up, and he said, 'Oh, what a load you have taken off my mind! I'm so glad I sent you.'

I may add that no notice was taken of this escapade, and we were almost immediately sent to Cork for embarkation to the Mediterranean, and we embarked on board the man-of-war *Simoon* for the Ionian Islands.

CHAPTER 8

Four months in Florence

Our old quartermaster, Mr. Benson, had just been promoted to be paymaster in another regiment, and so we had a new quartermaster.

He turned out to be a terrible duffer, and in consequence I volunteered to perform his duty and superintend the embarkation of everything.

The colonel gladly accepted the offer, and the whole of the baggage being piled on carts, I started off with an escort to the *Simoon.*

A tug took us alongside as the ship was lying at anchor in Cork Harbour, I having arranged that all the officers' baggage that they required during the voyage was duly to be marked 'Cabin.'

First, I selected all the officers' cabins, and I took care that each servant should know which was his master's luggage; then, as the baggage was sent down from deck, everything marked 'Cabin' was taken possession of by the servants for their masters—everything else went to the hold. Then I went to the main-deck, where the men were to be quartered. Now, imagine the main-deck of the ship as a long room, with tables and benches all along each side, close together, and one can form a very fair idea of what the place looked like.

There was just enough room for the men to sit back to back. Overhead were a series of shelves for the men's knapsacks, and at the head of each table was a rack to hold twelve muskets. Knowing exactly how many men we had to accommodate, I began at one end, marking on the first table with a piece of chalk, 'Grenadiers, twelve men,' and so on right round until the whole regiment was provided with sitting room, each company by itself, the companies being numbered from one to eight. In those days we had a grenadier company on the right and the Light Company on the left. These have since been abolished, but then we had them, and as Tom the barber used to say in India,

'All big men go grenadiers, handsome men Light Company,' as the captain of the Light Company had the pick of the regiment. This was my company for years.

Next morning the regiment was brought on board by tugs, and as I had a free hand to do just as I chose, I ordered up the grenadiers first, made every man sit down in his place at the tables already chalked, putting his musket in the rack and his knapsack overhead, and in a very short time I had every man in his place. I had just finished when the general and his staff came on board. Colonel Staunton received him at the gangway. The general looked very much surprised, and his first question was, on looking round the empty deck, 'Where is your baggage, colonel?'

'All below, sir.'

'What! already?' said the general in surprise, and his next question was, 'Where is the regiment?'

'In their quarters, general, on the main-deck.'

Then the general proceeded down the ladder. The word 'Attention!' was given, and the regiment rose to a man amid profound silence, everyone in his place. The general remarked, 'I've never seen an embarkation like this before in my life; it does you the highest credit, colonel, and I shall take care to make it known at headquarters.

So much for a little organisation. The whole thing was perfectly simple.

Captain, afterwards Admiral, Kincome, commanded the *Simoon*. The British Navy at this time was at a very low ebb, and economy had almost run mad. Apparently, every pound of coals was grudged by the authorities, and, as she was a full-rigged ship with only a miserable little screw, we had to sail whenever there was a breath of wind. The crew were the most miserable specimens that I have ever seen on a ship. They could scarcely set or take in a sail, and poor Captain Kincome was nearly driven out of his senses. I have seen him shouting for an hour before he could get a studdingsail set.

When we got into the Bay of Biscay, we had a dreadful time of it. The ship rolled frantically and tumbled about; the sea spouted in at all the portholes, so that our cabins were full of water, and, to make matters still worse, the hatches were all battened down, almost hermetically sealed, so that there was an entire want of ventilation. Not a breath of air could get at us, and for nearly three days and nights we were breathing the foulest of air, and nearly everyone was deadly seasick at the same time. It was worse, if possible, than the Black Hole of

Calcutta of historic memory. How we lived is almost a mystery, and I look back still upon these days with the greatest horror.

Nothing very remarkable happened until we passed Gibraltar, when the captain decided to take a short-cut through the Straits of Messina.

The navigation was so erratic that a small island which we were told we should pass four miles to the north was actually passed two miles to the south. Then they could not find the Straits of Messina, and nearly ran on shore into a bay on the coast of Italy. Fortunately, it was quite calm, and we were going under steam at the time. The ship was stopped, charts consulted, and they found that we had run in amongst a number of dangerous rocks, so we had to steam slowly out stern foremost. Eventually we discovered the Straits, passed through, and arrived safely at Corfu, where the general ordered the regiment to proceed to Zante. So, we started quietly under sail, and while we were approaching the extreme end of the island of Santa Mora, known in classics as Sappho's Leap, a heavy swell was running, and the waves were breaking wildly on the perpendicular cliff. Soon it fell a dead calm, and the captain ordered the fires to be lighted to get up steam.

What was our horror to see that we were slowly and surely drifting on to these rocks! The captain frantically shouted to the engineer to get up steam as fast as possible, but of course that was a matter of time, as the fires were not even lighted. Three or four times he rushed to the hatchway to shout to the engineer if the steam was ready; the reply came, 'Not yet, sir.' By this time only two waves intervened between us and the rocks. Two or three minutes more would have seen a fearful tragedy, when the screws revolved, and we crept slowly, but safely, away. In due time we landed at Zante.

Before going further, I must recall one incident that occurred during the passage out. There was a subaltern who was very much disliked by his brother-officers, who consequently often used to play practical jokes on him. I am happy to say that I was not one of the number. The cabins were all fitted with Venetian blinds for the sake of ventilation, so it was easy for the youngsters to insert the nozzle of a syringe through the Venetians and give him a shower. I was walking up and down the deck one day, and had not the least idea that anything was going on below. I ran down the ladder to go to my cabin, and as I walked briskly along a sword was plunged through the Venetian with great force, and grazed my chest. One moment sooner and I should have been a dead man.

This was the only disagreeable affair that occurred during the passage, and my 'Friend of the Drawn Sword' left the regiment shortly after our arrival at Zante. We used to have great fun in the evenings; the sailors were 'piped' to skylark, and the band came on the quarter-deck and played country dances, etc., for the amusement of the men and sailors. There was one very fine sailor on board, standing over six feet in his stockings, and I used sometimes to put on a gown and an old mutch cap and dance as his partner. The figures were danced by order, and not in any regular succession, as would be the case on shore, and when the order came, 'Every man ride his chum,' my partner jumped on my back and was trotted round the deck amidst shouts of laughter.

One night it came on to blow hard, and while we were at mess, I heard the captain order, 'Double reef topsails.' In those days we had to dine in full dress—scarlet coat and epaulettes. I ran up on deck just as I was, and went up on to the mizzen-yard with the sailors to help reefing, to the no small surprise of the men, who had no idea that I was an old sailor. When coming down again I was pounced upon by two of the men to tie me in the rigging for my 'footing.'

I simply said, 'It's all right; I am an old hand, and you shall have your "footing." So, we all came down together, and in due time I fulfilled my promise. Next day we set a delightful trap for my 'Friend of the Sword,' as I shall call him. Having first given a hint to the sailors, one of the officers offered to bet him that he could not go up the rigging as far as the mizzen-top and come down again within five minutes. Up went our friend very cautiously, and, just as he got near the top, two sailors, like monkeys, ran up behind him and tied him to where he was. Then the officer who made the bet pulled out his watch calmly and announced that the five minutes were up! Of course, no money passed hands, but he had to pay his 'footing.'

Shortly after our arrival we had a visit from a Captain Blakely who had left the army in disgust, being (as he maintained he was) the original inventor of the now celebrated Armstrong gun, having furnished full particulars of the invention to the War Office months before Armstrong appeared on the scene. The War Office took no notice of him whatever, and we can therefore appreciate his disgust at his treatment.

As he knew Italy well, I got four months' leave, and we went together to Florence, when he introduced me to the British Society of the city. Amongst others was Charles Lever, the celebrated novelist, who always had an 'at home' one day in every week. The Austrians were in possession of Florence at this time, and a large garrison was quartered in the town.

One of the cavalry officers one day purchased a very fine charger, which neither he nor any man in the regiment could ride, the animal had such a fierce and ungovernable temper—at least, so they said—so he was sold for an 'old song,' as the saying is. Lever's eldest daughter bought him, and mastered him at once, not by whip and spur, but by kindness. She was a magnificent horsewoman, and shortly after this there was a grand review, and Miss Lever rode her horse down to the parade. You may imagine the disgust of the officer when he saw her riding down the ranks on the animal which every man in the regiment knew so well.

I passed a very happy four months in Florence. I had apartments with a family where I had arranged to be treated like one of themselves, this for the purpose of acquiring the language more rapidly. Immediately after breakfast I had the services of an Italian teacher, then dined in the middle of the day, and generally went on horseback to the casino, where all the beauty and fashion assembled in the afternoon to hear the band play.

I must relate one little incident:

In apartments in the same house Marcellina Lotti resided with her father and mother. She was the *prima donna* at the opera. I took a stall there, and used often to go and hear her, and we became very good friends. For weeks it had been announced that a very great man was to sing at a concert supported by the whole strength of the opera company. Tickets were a fabulous price, and all were disposed of long before the day arrived. I had no intention of going, but as I was running upstairs in the evening I accidentally met 'Lotti' coming down in full costume. She asked me, 'Are you not coming?' and I replied, 'No.'

'Oh! you shall come.'

'But,' I said, 'I have no ticket.'

'Never mind,' she answered; 'go and dress, and come immediately. You have just time. Drive to the door, and when you get there ask for Signor So-and-so. I'll give him his orders.'

Accordingly, I went, was received with extreme politeness, and was ushered up into a beautiful drawing-room, which was full of company consisting of all the great singers of Florence who were to do honour to the great man. It appeared to me that people took an unusual interest in my arrival. I heard a great deal of talking, but I thought nothing of it, and sat quietly talking to 'Lotti' and her friends on a sofa.

Soon a door was thrown open at the end of the room. This led into a gallery which opened into the concert-hall. The immense hall was packed; this I could see at a glance. Before I well knew how it happened, I was politely seized—I may say, in spite of all my protests, was ceremoniously escorted into the gallery at the head of the procession. In a moment terrific applause burst from the whole audience, and to my horror I discovered that they thought I was the great man of the evening! Of course. I bowed and bowed again. I could do nothing else, and dived into a back seat as soon as possible. Then the great man himself came forward and was not received with half the enthusiasm with which I was, but I could hear some people laughing as they realized what had happened.

At the expiry of my leave I returned to my regiment, and shortly afterwards I received notice that my yacht, the *Lizzie*, had arrived at Malta. The *Lizzie* had been purchased by a friend for me from the Great Western Yacht Club. My instructions were for a good sea-boat that would stand all weathers, and not a racer. I had no difficulty in getting leave to go and fetch her, so I went by the first steamer up to Corfu, when Campbell of the 71st offered to take me over to Malta in his yacht the *Pet*; so with the assistance of the barrack-master, Major Munro, I engaged a skipper and two hands, Italians, who were domiciled at Corfu. All the yachts of the garrison were manned by these men, who were splendid sailors and thoroughly trustworthy. I am afraid I cannot say the same for the Greeks.

We started off, and as it was summer-time we had very light winds. We were eleven days altogether on the passage, but when off Cape Spartivento, which is on the coast of Italy, a fierce storm got up, and a heavy sea made the old *Pet* tumble about in a most uncomfortable manner.

I stuck to the tiller all night, and when, as we were running before the wind, a heavier sea than usual washed the compass clean away, I had to steer by the stars till we had it mounted again.

In the morning we arrived at Catania, which is at the foot of Mount Etna, so we ran into the harbour, having resolved to ascend the mountain—14,000 feet high. We went straight to the British Consul, who gave us every information and a letter of introduction to Signor Jemilaro, who lived in the highest village on the mountain, and who was quite an authority on eruptions in general, and on Mount Etna in particular, having studied it all his life and written a book on the subject, a copy of which he presented to me.

As the correct thing was to see the sunrise from the summit of the mountain, we did not start till it was dark, with a mule each to ride, and two guides. The mules evidently knew the road, so we had no trouble with them.

Sometime well on in the night we dismounted in a forest of trees, lighted a fire, and had a good supper, and waited till the guides told us it was time to start. We rode up and up in the dark for a long time; I have no idea how long, but high above all the trees.

At last the guides told us to dismount, and one man led the mules away to take shelter, we were told, in a cave. The remaining guide led us along still in the dark to what appeared to be a nearly level plateau of frozen snow. Here I had one or two disagreeable tumbles, and I soon found out that wherever a piece of black cinder rested on the ice (for the snow was literally ice), the heat of the sun melted a round hole in the snow, sometimes 1 foot or 18 inches deep, and stepping into one of these holes you were bound to come down. So, for the rest of the walk I avoided black spots. After a time, we arrived at a ruined hut, called the Casa Inglesi, intended for a shelter for the British tourists.

We now tackled the crater itself, which was a huge cone of very soft sand, almost perpendicular, probably 1,000 feet high.

As you stepped up your foot came back again, and so it was altogether a most tiresome climb. The worst of it was that the heat from the ground was so great that we were bathed in perspiration, and every now and then, by way of a change, an icy cold wind blew upon us. Of course, we had on very thin garments, as the month of August in the Mediterranean Sea is by no means cool.

Once arrived at the top, the ground was so frightfully hot that we could not attempt to sit down, exhausted as we were, and the fumes of the sulphur were quite overpowering. The crater was quite open, and as we stood on the narrow lip, we could see the puffs of steam and sulphur-smoke shooting out at the bottom, a long way down. In some places on the lip of the crater the sulphur so predominated that it was actually on fire. It was altogether about as uncomfortable a situation as one can imagine. The guide had a frightfully narrow escape. The ground under his feet suddenly gave way and shot down into the crater, and it was a miracle he did not go down with it.

Notwithstanding that our feet were almost burned, we remained there until we saw the sun rise, and two things struck me particularly: one was that as the sun rose it cast a distinct shadow of the mountain on the western sky; and the other was that as you looked down you could realize the tremendous height you were up, but in looking straight away towards the western horizon, it appeared on a level with the eye.

The effect was very remarkable, and as the morning was beautifully clear, the outline of Italy was exactly like the well-known boot, as we used to call it at school. It did not take us long to run down what had been such a fearful climb up, across the level snow-plain once more, from which I sketched the crater. I have the sketch still. Then we went back to the mules, and thence down to the harbour in our carriage, after twenty-six hours of hard work without any rest. I turned in at once, fell into a deep sleep immediately, from which I did not wake for about eighteen hours, till the forenoon of the next day.

When I went on deck we were out of sight of land and well on our way to Malta, and they told me that they had had a gale and a calm while I was asleep, all of which I was totally unconscious of. I was particularly anxious as to our whereabouts, as we were out of sight of land, and I was the only one on board that had the slightest knowledge of navigation.

Fortunately, the *Pet's* skipper had got the correct course to Malta given to him from some kindly captain before leaving the port.

In due time we arrived at Malta, dropped anchor in the Admiralty Harbour, and almost immediately Admiral Houston Stewart, then the owner of the *Gart* at Callander, came off in his barge, which was longer than our little cutter, though not quite so high out of the water.

He stepped on board—a fine, jovial sailor, and by no means a light weight—went down with some difficulty into our little cabin, and sat and laughed till we could feel the *Pet* shaking all over. 'Oh,' he exclaimed, 'you soldier officers are a queer lot. There's not an officer in the British Navy would come over in such a thing as this from Corfu.' And then he laughed again. As he knew my friends very well, he took us off with him on shore, and hospitably entertained us during our stay at Malta. His son was then Captain Houston Stewart, in command of the *Modeste*, stationed at Corfu, and we afterwards became great friends. I had the pleasure of a fortnight's cruise on board the *Modeste*.

My own yacht, the *Lizzie*, was lying dismantled not far off, so I put my crew on board and set them to work to bend the sails and get all ready for sea. Just before we were ready to start a Mr. Pell came to see me, and said that I would be doing him and Major Brookes (whom I knew very well as the commanding Royal Engineer at Zante) a great favour if I would give a passage to two servant-maids who had been 'eating their heads off' in Malta for the last three months, as there was no communication between the two places. After some demur I consented and told him that I purposed sailing on the evening of the next day.

Campbell and I had arranged that we were to sail back in company to Zante, going direct instead of the roundabout way we came.

The two officers belonging to the garrison were particularly anxious to be taken with us, so I consented to take Captain Thursby, and Campbell took the other one. Campbell, with the *Pet*, instead of waiting for me, started off in the forenoon, and was soon out of sight.

I may mention that the *Lizzie* had two cabins, two sofa-berths in the main cabin, and two good berths in the after-cabin, with looking-glass and wash-hand basin and lamps complete. The companion-stairs separated the two cabins, so I fitted up the after-cabin for Major Brookes's servants. In the dusk of the evening, after waiting for some time for Mr. Pell, we got up the anchor and started. It was now quite dark, with a very light air; and just as we were stealing out of the harbour a boat came alongside, some luggage was hastily put on board, and Pell handed two parties on deck, one tall and the other short. The tall party was introduced to me as Mrs. Woods, Major Brookes's housekeeper, and Mrs. Woods introduced me to her niece (H)emma, and before I could look round Mr. Pell and his boat had disappeared into the darkness.

Mrs. Woods sat in profound dignity on the skylight beside (H)emma. After a little while I suggested to her that she had better go downstairs to her cabin. 'Oh, thank you,' was the answer, 'it's not worthwhile.' Then she turned to me and said, 'Where is the steamboat?'

I said, 'What steamboat?'

'Why,' she replied, 'the steamboat that's to take us to Zante.'

'Why,' I said, 'you're going in my cutter to Zante.'

At this she started up and almost screamed, 'In this thing? Oh, I shall be drowned! I shall be drowned! Let me out, let me out!'

I said to her, 'Why are you afraid of being drowned?' Pointing to the crew, I continued: 'You see these men? Well, they've all got their wives and families at home. Do you think they want to be drowned?'

Then she started again: 'Oh, that Pell, the villain, the scoundrel! He told us that we were going in a larger steamer than the P. and O. that brought us from England. Oh, the scoundrel, if I had him!'—clenching her fists at the same time. After a while she cooled down, and soon consented to go down with 'Hemma.' I introduced them to their cabin, which was really larger than the sleeping berths of the P. & O. in those days, and they had good ventilation from the skylight overhead. As was my habit, I remained on deck all night when out of sight of land. In the morning we were stealing along with a light breeze. The skipper suggested that we should try the pump to see if she were water-tight.

So, the pump was rigged, and a bucket of water poured in to make it draw, and then *jig-jog* went the handle. I was steering at the time, and suddenly I heard a commotion down below. All at once up rushed Mrs. Woods in her nightdress, with her hair flying wildly in the wind, the very picture of terror. Down she flopped on her knees, and clasping her hands in the air, called out in a loud voice, 'Oh dear! oh dear! they've taken to the pumps, and we are all going to the bottom!'

The faces of the crew were a picture to see, and I called out, 'It's all right, Mrs. Woods; we're not going to the bottom yet.' Then she suddenly realised the situation, jumped up, and scuttled back to her cabin as fast as she came out.

Now to return to the *Pet*. She sailed in the forenoon of the day on which we left in the afternoon, and was soon out of sight; but the next morning, shortly after Mrs. Woods's adventure, we fell in with Campbell again. The officer and Campbell came on board and stayed with us till the evening, and we arranged to keep together all the way back to Zante, the *Lizzie* leading the way. As the latter was by far the faster boat, I had to sail with reduced canvas all night with a lantern hung over the stern for the benefit of the *Pet*. This I had promised to do.

About daylight I went below and turned in. I had only just fallen asleep when Spero, my skipper, came down and told me that the *Pet* had 'gone about.' I immediately went on deck, and there she was 'gone about,' and sailing right away west while we were heading east. In the clear light of the morning I could see the top of Mount Etna in the extreme distance, and this evidently accounted for my friend's departure. I found out afterwards that while Campbell and his friend were asleep, his skipper, evidently in a funk at being out of sight of land, was overjoyed to see Mount Etna, and had steered straight for it, telling Campbell in the morning that I had run away from him in the night.

His voyage after this was most unfortunate. They ran along the coast of Sicily, and by some extraordinary feat of navigation arrived at Naples instead of Corfu. Sad to relate, his companion on board was seized with cholera and died there. How Campbell got back I never quite knew, but he laid the whole blame on me, and I had some trouble in vindicating my character by proving the facts of the case and by the production of my log-book, in which everything was carefully recorded, with the evidence of my crew.

Captain Thursby got the steamer from Zante to Constantinople, and so everything passed off satisfactorily as far as I was concerned. I think I forgot to mention that I brought over three enormous sacks of letters and newspapers for the whole of the Ionian Islands, as all communication between Malta and the Islands had been cut off for some months—a grand stroke of economy. The steamer which had regularly carried the mails for a subsidy of £25,000 a year had been dispensed with, to the infinite inconvenience and annoyance of everyone concerned. I, through my own colonel, offered to run the mail once a month between Malta and Corfu, making up all my duties as well. This offer, as something quite unheard of, was declined, without thanks, by the authorities at Corfu. So much for red-tape.

One of our great sources of amusement was going over to the mainland of Greece to shoot woodcock. I should like to give one of my experiences of such a trip.

Four of us got a fortnight's leave with strict injunctions to be back on a certain day to allow others to have their turn.

Our destination was a monastery, and our party consisted of two brother officers and myself, and I took Joe Brown, my servant, to clean the guns and make himself generally useful. We had an Italian also with us who was a good cook, and who spoke English and Greek fluently.

A Greek monastery is much more like a castle than anything else. What we should call the ground-floor was strong masonry without windows or doors, and to enter the convent you had to go up a solid flight of stone steps with a square landing on the top, to what one may call the first-floor. These stairs were built 6 feet away from the wall of the house, so that when you arrived at the top you had to turn short round to the left across a small drawbridge to get to the door. There was a loophole on each side of the door, so that any person on the landing could be shot at once; and when the drawbridge was up, they could not even get at the door to break it in. We were in a large room with windows, which held no glass. In one corner was a delightful graven image with a lamp burning before it, night and day, and I well remember that the unfortunate man whose bed was in that corner found himself before morning well smudged with oil dripping from the lamp.

We had a splendid fortnight's shooting, and arranged to start in good time to catch the steamer which was to take us back from Prevesa.

As bad luck would have it, in the morning, when we were prepared to start, there was a perfect deluge of rain, and the men and ponies who were to take our baggage positively refused to stir, as they said there were several rivers without bridges, which it would be impossible to take our impedimenta across. Here was a nice fix to be in. If we waited it meant losing the steamer, and we resolved to go at all hazards. So, leaving everything we had in charge of the abbot, with a stick in our hands and a revolver buckled round our waists, we started. We soon came to a river in heavy flood which we must swim. Then the question was, what were we to do with Joe Brown, who could not swim a stroke? So, we proceeded without stripping (which would have been utterly useless in our wet state) to wade in, after tying our revolvers on the top of our heads with our pocket-handkerchiefs.

There was only a short distance in the middle which was really out of our depth, so the others, leaving me with Joe, swam across. Then they broke off the largest branch of a tree they could find, and one of them came back into the river until he was almost up to the neck, and held out the branch. It was too short by a long way, so I made Joe get on my back and hold tight round my neck, and we waded in together. Soon I lost my footing, and after a desperate struggle in attempting to swim with Joe on my back, I caught hold of the branch, and we were triumphantly towed on shore.

We proceeded on our way, but sometime after this a fearful thunderstorm set in, and a thunderbolt came down, struck an old oak-tree in front of us, and split a huge branch, which fell right across the road within a few yards of us. All day we trudged along a very bad footpath—we could not call it a road—and I remember asking Joe if he were tired, to which he pluckily replied, 'Oh no, sir, but I've a terrible pain in my legs,' which was much the same thing.

About dusk we came to what may be called a house of entertainment, and as a great favour we were allowed to take possession of a room upstairs, perfectly empty, but with a large hearthstone, and, of course, no grate or anything else. We soon had a roaring fire on the hearth, and we proceeded to pull off our clothes and wring them. Being frantically hungry, we asked for something to eat. We certainly did not ask for anything to drink, and the only thing that the landlord could give us was an enormous dish of fried onions. When he came in we took good care to be cleaning up our revolvers, as without them we would have had a very good chance of having our throats cut before morning, and we had just to put on our half-dried clothes, lie down in front of the fire and sleep till daylight.

The next day was bright and clear, and we continued our journey, got to Prevesa in time for the steamer, and so rejoined the regiment before our leave was up, none the worse for our adventure. This is what I call 'roughing it.' Many people who talk about 'roughing it' do not know what the words mean.

From Zante I was sent with my company to Santa Mora, and had the pleasure of seeing again Sappho's Leap, where we had nearly our last leap on board the *Simoon*.

Swettenham, now a general, was my subaltern, and we had quartered with us in the fort an artillery officer, Lieutenant Waller, and a staff doctor. We had a delightful winter, with no one to trouble us, and no communication with the outer world except by a steamer which called every Saturday morning, bringing our letters and receiving our correspondence.

With the help of the yacht, we soon came to know the whole country around us, both Turkey and Greece, and had plenty of good shooting.

Swettenham and I had many adventures together. He may recall the manner of his meeting me on my return to Zante from Malta, when Mrs. Woods and 'Hemma' were my passengers. He was taking his morning swim, when, spying my yacht at anchor, he struck out for her. Imagine his feelings when, on reaching the *Lizzie*, he saw two ladies awaiting him! He turned round and made for the shore. Next time he brought his clothes with him!

When sent from Balaclava to the front, we found the mess very short of things. Transport being in a state of chaos, we annexed an old cart lying deserted on the road, and harnessed four of our ponies to it with old ropes. Swettenham and myself dressed as privates, Swaffield as a corporal, and we made a pompous little officer command us in full uniform.

Off we started, the men of the first battery that we passed roaring with laughter at our turn-out, as they took us for privates!

Arrived at the regimental store, we found the sergeant in charge absent, so began loading up. Swaffield took the liberty of opening a bottle of beer, which was at his mouth when the sergeant, rushing in, seized him by the throat, exclaiming, 'You villain!' then stood aghast, recognising an officer!

CHAPTER 9

Departure for the Crimea

This was the celebrated cold first winter of the Crimean War. I saw the snow lying on the beach, and the lagoon to the south of the fort, although salt water, was completely frozen over on one occasion—the only time that I have ever seen salt water frozen. It was an amusing sight to watch the gulls walking on the ice, and their astonishment, when they dabbed their heads down to pick up anything, at coming in contact with the hard ice.

The outer ditch of the fort was used as a quarantine station, a horrid place that only Greeks could have thought of putting anyone in. One morning it was reported to me that a Hungarian doctor was in quarantine. I had him up into the fort at once, as I never would obey the ridiculous quarantine laws, and found that he was going to join the Turkish Army and was to proceed to Prevesa at once, but the Greeks' idea was to keep the poor fellow for a fortnight in quarantine, fleece him well, and then make him pay a fabulous price for the hire of a boat, as there was no communication between the two places. So, I took him over to the *pasha* at Prevesa in the *Lizzie*. The *pasha* was most grateful, and highly appreciated my kindness to this doctor. I may mention that the doctor had his wife and daughter with him, which would have made things all the more disagreeable had he remained in quarantine.

No vessel was allowed to pass up or down after dark to or from the Gulf of Arta, but I got leave to come and go just as I liked. I must give another shooting adventure. On one occasion we started off to shoot, at a place we had not visited before, at the far end of a big lake. Accordingly, we set out, my two companions walking round with their guns to shoot while I took charge of the boat with the tents and everything required for a week's stay in a country of which it might

117

be said it was uninhabited. The Greek population was very small, and you could wander for days without coming across a house or a habitation, or any signs of cultivation; in fact, there was no such thing to be seen as a solitary house, and the natives lived in small communities for mutual protection.

Having arrived at the other end of the lake, and on getting out of the boat, what was my surprise to find that I was on a floating island which was, however, quite solid to stand upon on the lake side! The water was very deep—indeed, I could not reach the bottom with a pole, but I could put it underneath, as it were, the land, which proved that it was floating. I took the pole in my hand by the middle, à la Blondin, and proceeded to investigate.

I found that the island very soon thinned out, and I sunk through it, but with the help of the pole held crossways I scrambled out again only wet up to the waist, and I found that there were some 200 or 300 yards between where I was and the real shore. I coasted round up and down along the face of the so-called island, every now and then finding an opening which did not pass through, so after forcing the boat in I had to force it out again and try another place.

Darkness set in, and my companions on the shore were firing their guns and shouting, 'Why don't you come?' as they could hear us but could not see in the darkness what was going on. For several hours we fought and struggled on, trying either to get round the island or through it. After some time of fighting and struggling, and being wet through from several ugly plunges in the weeds, we managed to land, and the night being cold, as it was winter-time, it was anything but a pleasant situation. Our friends told us that the whole country in the immediate vicinity was under water, but that they had found a small dry mound some little distance away.

We tied the boat to a tree, each one seized as much as he could carry, and we staggered off, splashing through the darkness till we arrived at the mound in question, and, having cut down two or three trees and made a roaring fire, we pitched our tents about 2 a.m., after enjoying a good hot supper, and lay down. We had scarcely fallen asleep, when one of the party began to shout loudly. We thought, naturally, that robbers were upon us, so we struck a light and seized our arms.

We saw the individual in question sitting up on his bed, looking the very picture of horror, and declaring that his bed was jumping up and down. On removing the bed, we found that he had been sleeping on a large tortoise, which objected to the load, so we soon set things to rights by turning it out.

After a good week's sport, we went down to the sea to return home, and found one of the *Lizzie's* men with the small boat waiting for us; but as most of the way back was through a lagoon, we did not mind being a little overloaded. The last mile or two, however, was through a passage in the reef and across the open sea to Santa Mora. As it was a dead calm we decided to go through a narrow opening in the reef as a short cut. When we got near this opening, although there was not a breath of wind, we found there was a heavy swell rolling in, and thundering on the reef in white foam.

The question was, should we go through, or should we turn back? The decision was to chance it, and a very close chance it was.

As we shot through, a great wave caught the boat and threw us back almost on the reef. As the wave sank down with the boat in the hollow, the stern just missed the point of the rock by about 6 inches. Had we touched it the boat would have been instantly capsized, and nothing could have saved one of us, as there was a fierce current rushing through the passage, so that we could not have got back again into the calm water, and swimming could not have saved us, as we should have had four miles to swim.

The current fortunately took the boat a yard or two clear of the rocks, and although the next wave threw us back—the boat being almost perpendicular in the air—and the crest of the wave rushing over us filling us nearly full of water, the current again brought us clear of the breakers, and with a few strokes of the oar we were perfectly safe beyond the broken water, and were merely bobbing up and down on a heavy swell. It was an uncommonly narrow escape of our lives, but we got home safely. I may mention that it was dark when we arrived at the opening, which added very much to the danger of the situation. Swettenham's oar was unshipped by the sea also, which made matters worse.

While quartered in the Ionian Islands, the garrison at Corfu decided upon having a regatta.

Of course, I took the *Lizzie* up at once and entered her for the Cup Race. Twenty-two yachts in all entered; I have the list now.

The *Lizzie* and two others were the three largest cutters entered for the race. All the others had a time allowance so liberal that they would have beaten us easily had it not been that the wind fell just after we rounded the turning-point (a boat) in a race of twenty-two miles, and all the little yachts were left becalmed, while the *Lizzie* and the cutter belonging to the Lord High Commissioner, Sir Henry Ward, were the only two that kept the wind.

The town of Corfu is magnificently protected: a rocky island in front strongly fortified, and on the mainland a powerful battery commanding each entrance to the anchorage—a most splendid harbour with deep water, and where a whole fleet could remain in perfect safety. It was a very great mistake giving this island up to the Greeks.

To return to the race. We started at the north end of the island. A boat anchored about ten miles away was the turning-point, and the winning-post was the *Modeste*, man-of-war; we had to pass between her and the island.

We started with a fair wind, and the poor *Lizzie* had a very poor chance against the tremendous balloon sails of some of the other yachts. We only had our usual rig, which was intended for all weathers. Notwithstanding this disadvantage, we passed all the small craft and rounded the turning-point almost at the same time as the Lord High Commissioner's cutter. Now came one of the most exciting races on record.

While it fell dead calm, to the exclusion of all the small craft, we stole away with a light breeze which gradually increased to half a gale. The *Lizzie* tore along close-hauled with the other yacht rather ahead, but about 100 yards to leeward. We could barely hold our course close-hauled, but we rushed along with the gunwale almost under water, making a bee-line for the southern part of the island, round which we had to go. My antagonist, for we were now all alone, luffed off every now and then when a hard squall struck us, with a view of getting to windward of me, but every time he did so he lost a little way, and as we neared the island, I was leading by a few yards.

My subaltern, who was on board with me, was lying flat on his face on the deck in such a state of excitement that he could not stand up, calling out every now and then, 'Are we gaining? Are we gaining?'

When we rounded the south end of the island it was a fair beat up to the *Modeste*. When I was on the last tack I found to my great disgust that I could not weather her, so, rounding as close as possible, I shouted to the crew to stand fast, which for a moment flabbergasted them completely, and, knowing what the *Lizzie* could do, I put the helm down and cleared the winning-post by about 2 yards in the forereach, and won the race by four seconds. The tiller had never left my hands from start to finish.

The captain of the other yacht thought that he had won, as he was lying high enough to clear the *Modeste's* bows, and in his excitement after the pistol went off, he ran into the *Modeste's* jib-boom and carried away her topmast.

The next little incident worth relating is connected with the arrival of Abdi Pasha, the Governor of Albania, and his suite, on his way to Constantinople to take part in the Russo-Turkish war. As a matter of course, he was put into quarantine in the ditch of the fort, and also, as a matter of course, I brought him up to the fort with his suite, which consisted of a smart young Turkish officer and a magnificent Albanian chief in his white kilt and national costume, with, as Swettenham described it, 'pistols and daggers hung all over him.'

I was told afterwards that he slept on his bed in full costume, without laying aside any of his weapons. This must give one an idea of the wild sort of life he lived. Abdi patted him on the back and introduced him to me as a first-rate man to loot a village!

The first amusing incident which I remember was, that when dinner was announced, my man Joe Brown, who has already appeared on these pages, was got up for the occasion, dressed in full mess costume blue coat, white facings and white stockings all complete. He politely motioned Abdi to his chair, to which Abdi replied, 'No, your Excellency, that is your seat,' then took him by the shoulders and put him in the chair! Joe's face was a picture. However, I soon set matters right.

The next funny incident was after the fish, to which we used our forks only, the Turks looking on without partaking. Then a plate of roast beef was put before the *aide-de-camp*, and he immediately began to copy us with his fork only, hunting the beef all over the plate. I saw him glance at me, and in a moment was sharp enough to notice that I had a knife in my hand, and he immediately picked his up and went to work like a man.

After dinner Abdi proceeded to let us see him perform the celebrated feat of cutting a silk handkerchief in two in the air. This trick he did several times. I afterwards showed him the common race-course trick of 'prick the garter,' which excited him terribly, as he always missed it.

Then he ordered the Albanian chief to try his luck, and he succeeded no better than his master. Having had the trick explained, all parties were delighted.

Before we parted in the evening, I presented Abdi with a pair of plated English hunting-spurs, and buckled them on his boots. He was hugely delighted, and declared that he would never part with them. The only thing I ever heard of Abdi afterwards was that he got the worst of it in a fight with the Russians in Asia Minor.

In the morning he went out to the pier with his rifle, and had one egg after another dropped on the sea at a considerable distance; the egg bobbed up and down with the sea, but he smashed it every time.

Shortly before Christmas I had a visit from the English resident, who, of course, was the great man of the island, and who represented Her Majesty Queen Victoria.

He informed us that he had had a little diplomatic difficulty with some of the great people of the island, who announced that they would absent themselves from the great annual levee. To avoid this, he was going on a month's leave, and he requested me to take his place. This I did, and a most amusing day we had. We got up in full dress, and I had the artillery officer and doctor for my staff.

Swettenham commanded one guard of honour, and the police, who were in their best clothes, formed another. The Secretary of the Legation, or whatever it may be called, received us, and we proceeded to a hall, where I was seated on a raised platform with my staff behind me. The two guards of honour formed in line on each side of the front door, and soon I heard, 'Present arms!' and in walked an archbishop in full canonicals.

He was presented in due form, and, as previously instructed, I took his hand and placed him in a chair on my right. Then the presentation began, everybody who was anybody being presented, including the chief baker and butcher in the island. Then the schoolchildren tramped in, and at the word of command, 'Halt! Front! Salute!' every little hand went up to their caps.

Then the secretary, in a pretty little speech, informed me 'that these leetle children come to thank you as representing Her Gracious Majesty for the preevileges which they enjoy.'

Then 'queek' march, and out they went. I then presented my hand to the archbishop, and we headed a procession to the cathedral, where a service was beautifully performed, and the secretary, who remained at my elbow, informed me, 'Now they are praying for you.' Thus, ended the function, and we returned to barracks and proceeded to enjoy our Christmas dinner. Towards the end of it a merry party of my men rushed in and seized me, and carried me off shoulder-high to drink their health in the barrack-room. Unfortunately, they were not very steady on their legs, and in rushing downstairs we all went headlong together on to the barrack square. However, they soon picked me up again, and I got safely through the ordeal.

After that someone proposed to take a 6-pounder gun and have some practice on the beach. No sooner said than done. The men harnessed themselves to the gun, the back gate was opened, and out we trotted. A mark was put up at 200 or 300 yards away, and the gunner, as we called him, a lieutenant in the artillery, made such a bad shot that I chaffingly told him I would give him a shot at my jacket. He accepted the challenge, so I could not draw back, but marched down to the place, took my jacket off, knelt behind a small heap of stones about 18 inches high, and held the jacket up on the end of a walking-stick. He laid the gun carefully, *bang* it went, *whizz* came the shot, plumped into the heap of stones, kicking up a tremendous cloud of dust, and sending up the stones in all directions.

The moment the shot struck I jumped up and waved my jacket amid a burst of cheers. I then discovered that the shot had come clean through the heap of stones, and had been stopped by the last one. What would have happened if the last stone had not been there? We can only say, '*All's well that ends well*'; but it was a very foolish trick to play, both for the gunner and his target.

Nothing much occurred after this, till one morning early Joe rushed into my room to say that the *Lizzie* was wrecked inside the harbour. Sure enough a Greek brig had run into the *Lizzie* during the night as she lay at anchor, and there she was on the rocks. The windlass was capsized, the bowsprit driven right in, and the topmast carried away and hanging from the cross-trees. The whole fort had turned out. The men jumped into the water, and by main force got her off the rocks into deep water.

The authorities promptly boarded the brig and ordered the captain to pay compensation. This he refused to do, so they instantly took his rudder off and told him that when he paid fifty dollars compensation, he would get his rudder back again. This he did, after vowing vengeance on the *Lizzie*. I started off as soon as possible for Corfu to repair damages. The moment I was well out at sea the brig got under way, and followed us with every intention, I firmly believe, of murdering us. Most fortunately there was a head wind, and by beating to windward we gradually got away from them, but we had only the foresail and mainsail to help us.

At this time we had the order of readiness for the Crimea, and after I had put the *Lizzie* in perfect repair and a new topmast rigged, I sold her, with everything on board, to the colonel of one of the Militia regiments who had been sent out from England to relieve the garrison of the Ionian Islands. He took over the crew as well, so that I was relieved of all anxiety. Our parting from our good friends at Zante was most affecting. The 31st Regiment was greatly liked, and the Greeks were firmly under the impression that we would be annihilated by the Russians. Many men on the pier from which we embarked had the tears running down their cheeks, and the parting was, altogether, most touching.

CHAPTER 10

The First Assault on the Malakoff

We arrived in due course at Balaclava, disembarked, and were quartered there some time before proceeding to the front.

I shall not attempt to give any history of the campaign, but shall merely relate what I went through myself.

On one occasion, when we went down to duty, the whole of the men had been taken away in different directions. It was done in this way: 'One officer and 100 men wanted here;' 'One officer and 50 men wanted' in another place, and so on. Then they marched away, and Captain Swaffield and I were left behind with nothing to do. We found that our men were taken to open a fresh trench in a very exposed and dangerous position. It would have been extremely dangerous had the enemy discovered what they were doing, so the bright idea struck us, as we had nothing to do, to divert the enemy's attention.

We went into a quiet corner of the trenches where there was nobody, and commenced to hammer away on the stones with bits of old iron.

Soon the enemy discovered, as they thought, something very important going on, from the noise we were making. They opened a sharp fire in our direction, and, as we were pretty safe under the parapet, we kept up the tinkling noise, and thus drew the enemy's fire away from our men, so that they worked the whole night without a man being hit, and we considered we had done a very good night's work.

During the hot weather there was always an outcry for water for the men to drink, and there were everlasting complaints of the want of water. One night I went to General Wyndham, who was in charge of the trenches, and offered to be entirely responsible for the water-supply. He replied, 'Why, there's not an officer in the British Army would offer to do that! Are you really in earnest? For if you are, you may depend upon it your offer will be accepted, and I pity you.'

I replied, 'On one condition, that I do it my own way, and am not interfered with by anyone.' As a matter of fact, I carried out my offer with perfect satisfaction to everybody, but will explain my proceedings.

First of all I had a dozen zinc powder-magazines brought down and completely sunk into the earth with the mouths flush with the ground; the lids were strongly hinged on, and when closed were water-tight. From my knowledge of the trenches, I selected as safe a place as possible in a hollow, where nothing but an exploding shell could reach them. All this was done after I had command of the transport of the Second Division, and every morning I sent down a troop of ponies loaded with barrels of water, and had all the above magazines filled up. I soon found out how much water was really required, and took care that there was always plenty. I had a sentry placed in charge to prevent any man from using the water for washing, which they had constantly done up to this time.

Two or three days after I had fairly started all this, I got a line from the quartermaster-general of the division, laconic and to the point, 'The old story, no water!' I jumped on my horse and galloped right down to the trenches, left my horse in the twenty-one-gun battery, where there was good shelter, and walked down to the water depot. There I found about half the magazines quite empty, but the other half quite full; no sentry, however, was in charge! I rode straight back to the quartermaster-general's tent and told him how matters stood.

It appeared that a colonel in command of a party had sent up the report on the strength only of one of the men saying that there was no water, and he, I believe, got it very hot from the general for sending up such an unfounded report, without taking the trouble to first ascertain the facts. There was not another complaint made during the remainder of the siege, as there was always plenty of water, and the men knew where to go and get it without being allowed to waste it, which formerly had been done to a disgraceful extent.

As is now a matter of history, the transport of the army at this time reflected great disgrace, not on us who were on the spot, but on the home authorities. Words could not describe the hopeless confusion and stupidity connected with the whole department.

Colonel McMurdo, a most experienced and able officer, who had formerly been *aide-de-camp* to Sir Charles Napier in India (and married his daughter), was in command of the transport of the whole army, but very soon broke down from overwork. There were I don't know how many divisions of transport in command of officers picked up anyhow by the home authorities, many of them without the slightest idea of what they were expected to do when they got out, and no knowledge whatever of horses or wheel-carriages. Then the authorities applied to the Turkish Government for men to work the transport, and the system by which they were procured was quite delightful and refreshing.

A village, say, in Asia Minor, was surrounded by the Turkish troops, and nearly every able-bodied inhabitant seized, marched down to the sea, bundled on board a transport, and landed at Balaclava, handed over to one of the aforesaid officers, who was provided with an interpreter, and they were immediately formed into a division of transport, with two or three junior officers to assist. Then, as to the horses and mules which were required: they arrived in shiploads, having been purchased all over Europe with only rope halters round their heads, and so were taken possession of by the division. These animals were many of them quite unfit and savagely vicious, having evidently been got rid of by their former owners to their satisfaction.

Then, to complete the picture, shiploads of pack-saddles arrived, I know not from where, and were handed over for immediate use. Of course, no artificers were provided to fit the saddles, or harness, but they were simply put on the animals' backs, loaded at Balaclava with everything that was required for a large army, and sent up to the front, the result being frightful sore backs for the poor animals. Many of them were rendered utterly useless. The horseshoes provided came from Turkey, and were simply a flat plate of iron with a hole in the middle; and as some Turkish farriers were provided, they put them on after their own fashion, which I will describe.

The farrier took a good long rope, doubled it, and knotted a loop at the end to about the size of a good large horse-collar. This was put over the horse's head after the manner of a collar, the knot resting on the horse's chest. Then the two ends of rope were brought between his legs; each rope then taken by a man was hitched on to the fetlocks of his hind-legs and brought through the loop in front; then by a steady, hard pull the hind-legs were drawn up to the fore-legs, and the horse fell heavily on his side. All the four feet were then tied together by the fetlocks, the horse was propped up on his back, and the farrier sat down quietly beside him and proceeded to take off all the old shoes and put on new ones. When the work was finished his legs were untied, and he was allowed to get up again. No wonder that our farriers, when they came to shoe these animals, had great difficulty in doing

THE ATTACK ON THE MALAKOFF, 8TH SEPTEMBER, 1855

so, after the manner of civilized nations.

When the 31st landed at Balaclava, where we were quartered for some weeks—I presume to get acclimatised, as during that period we were never sent into the trenches, or took any part in the siege but every morning we had to march our companies into a wood—or, rather, I should call it a jungle, as there were no forest trees—every two or three men having an axe given to them to cut down branches. These were then carried to an open space, where the men set to work to make gabions, which they called 'crow's nests'; and you would hear in the morning a man calling out, 'It is "crow's-nests" again today, boys.' The gabions were made up by taking upright sticks about a yard long, sticking them in the ground, and then twisting branches basket-fashion, in and out, round them, up to the top, when they were pulled out and carried away ready for use.

To make a trench they were placed side by side, the earth dug out on the defender's side and filled into the gabions. More earth was then thrown out towards the enemy till a good solid bank was formed which could resist shot or shell. About 18 inches of solid ground was left between the gabions and the ditch, and on this the men could sit in perfect safety from direct fire, and when they required to fire them-selves, they had only to step up on to the place where they had been sitting, and fire over the top, exposing only the head and shoulders to the enemy. These sort of trenches we soon had an opportunity of test-ing for ourselves, crow's-nests and all.

One fine morning we marched up to the front, forming part of the Second Division of the army, and immediately a certain number of us were detailed for duty in the trenches. I was one of the party, and Eager was in command. Our route lay through a narrow valley known by the somewhat ominous title of the Valley of Death. Just as we turned out of the valley to climb up to the trenches, a shell came hopping down the ascent, bounded over our heads, and exploded in the air. No one was hit, but it was a very disagreeable introduction. When we got into the trenches we were handed over to the engineers for our night's work, and expected, of course, to be set to dig a fresh trench, as the British were sapping their way towards the redan. We had trenches both on our right and left flanks, forming a sort of semi-circle round the Russian fortifications.

My company was taken possession of by a corporal of Engineers, who escorted us some distance through the trenches into one that was empty, and there left us. We had not the slightest idea where we were or what we were expected to do! But a whisper had gone about that there was to be a bombardment in the morning. Hour after hour passed in silence, and just as daylight was coming in, a roar of artillery broke out behind us, and immediately the Russians responded. We found that we were right between the two fires, and shot and shell went screaming over our heads in both directions; the concussion was so great that small stones and earth came rolling down from the top of the trench. We simply sat still with our heads almost splitting from the fearful uproar. After about an hour of this the little corporal of Engineers put in an appearance and told us that we had been sent there by mistake, and we were to follow him immediately.

Away we went, and just as we got into what was called the 'twenty-one-gun battery,' one poor fellow was smashed by a round shot as he was passing an open embrasure which had only an empty gabion stuck in it to screen us from the enemy, but of course gave us no protection. Here I found the well-known and celebrated Colonel Gordon, the hero of Khartoum. He was sitting on a light camp-chair making notes, with a bright, happy smile on his face, while the shot and shell were flying about in all directions, as the bombardment was then at its fiercest. I shall never forget that noble face, of the most perfect composure in the midst of such imminent danger.

After a time, the ammunition became expended, and the bombardment gradually slackened off, and in a short while ceased altogether; then each side proceeded to fill up again until they had a sufficient supply for another artillery duel. All this time the French were steadily sapping forward their trenches to the Malakoff Tower, which was considered the key of the Russian position. Shortly after this they announced that they were prepared to make the assault, with our assistance. Of course, the 31st were duly marched down, and we were placed in reserve in rear of the twenty-one-gun battery, in such a position that we could see nothing of what was going on in the trenches. The attack commenced, and furious fighting went on for a long time, which ended in a repulse to the Allies all along the line, and we returned back to camp in the afternoon feeling very crestfallen after our defeat. This was on June 18, 1854.

It was after this that transport difficulties so increased that officers to take charge of it were in great demand. I volunteered my services, and was placed in command of the transport of the Second Division of the army with the local rank of major. Each battalion of the transport was known by a letter, and mine was the letter 'D,' all the animals being branded 'D' on the hip with a hot iron.

When I took command, I found it in charge of two sergeants. All the officers had from illness and overwork been invalided home, so it may be imagined what the state of affairs was I had to take charge of. Simply a mob of Turks with more mules and horses than they knew what to do with, and everything in the last stage of anarchy and confusion. I had no sooner pitched my tent than quite a mob of Turks appeared at the door. I asked a sergeant what it was all about.

'Oh,' he said, 'send them away, I never listen to them; send them away.'

I replied, 'Is there not an interpreter? Please find him.'

Then a shabby little Greek shuffled up and made a polite bow, and I proceeded to hear what the Turks had to say. The first man that came up began to speak and gesticulate wildly.

'Oh,' said the interpreter, 'that's a man that speaks a language no one understands, not even the Turks; but he makes energetic signs, which, I believe, mean that he wants to go home, as he is always pointing towards the south.'

Poor fellow! I wonder where the Turks caught him, but, of course, we shall never know. I had him shipped off with a good bag of sovereigns tied round his waist, as they were actually due to him as pay, and it was then that I got from the Turks themselves, through the interpreter, how they had enlisted. They came from a variety of districts in the Turkish Empire. I told them that they should go home as soon as possible, and at this they were greatly delighted. There were also in the battalion a good many Britishers who had been enlisted at home and sent out for transport duty. Many of them did not know a horse's head from his feet, and had never gone through any military drill; all the same they were armed with carbines and dressed in uniform.

Such was the state of affairs when I took over charge of the transport of the Second Division of the army. Fortunately, we had an able staff: Colonel Wilbraham (afterwards General commanding Netley Hospital) was our adjutant-general; Massey, afterwards Lord Clarina, who had been in the 31st with me, was also on the staff. I am sorry to say I forget the name of the quartermaster-general, but with his able assistance matters soon began to mend. Men volunteered from the different regiments of the division who had some knowledge of horses, and also some artificers. Shoeing-smiths, saddlers, and carpenters were found and handed over to me, and things began rapidly to get in better shape. I got officers, also, who were allowed to join from the different regiments.

One of them was Captain Pepper, in after-years my brother-in-law; and I also got the sergeant-major of the 31st presented with a commission, and made him my adjutant. He had served with me in the Light Company for years as my colour-sergeant, and I knew his excellent qualifications. He had been brought up in a hunting stable, and thoroughly understood the management of horses, and knew all about saddlery and harness—the very man made, as it were, for the situation—and a first-class rider; and now everything, comparatively speaking, was 'smooth sailing.'

September 8 was a day to be remembered, as on that day the Allied Forces made a combined attack and drove the Russians out of Sebastopol and across the harbour. Knowing what was about to take place, I rode quietly down to the trenches, which I well knew, having to visit them almost daily, and I arrived about an hour before the time fixed for the attack. I believe I was the only officer who at any time rode down to the trenches, it being considered rather dangerous, but the Russians never took any notice of me. I selected a favourable position to see everything, as I was quite free to go where I pleased. My only duty was to see a good supply of water taken into the redan, should it be captured; and I had a sergeant with a large party of ponies and barrels of water waiting in a ravine, not far off, for that purpose.

All was perfectly silent. The Russians knew quite well what was coming, and had prepared accordingly. I was looking over the parapet of the twenty-one-gun battery, which was comparatively high up, and commanded a perfect view both of our position and of Sebastopol. At the hour appointed the French suddenly appeared to rise out of the ground within a few yards of the Malakoff Tower. In a moment the Russians sprang into view and poured a fierce fire into the advancing French, which must have done fearful execution; but nothing checked the Frenchmen. They rapidly threw ladders across the ditch and swarmed into the fort. The battle raged in the town of Sebastopol till the late afternoon, with an incessant roar of musketry, but the Russians were driven back inch by inch, and were finally driven across the harbour. And now for the ugly side of the picture.

Our trenches were packed full of men, and simultaneously with the French attack on the Malakoff, quite a small party of red-coats rushed across the open space which divided our trenches from the redan.

This was the forlorn hope, but nobody followed them. They were led by General Wyndham in person, and they disappeared into the redan. It was here that 'Redan Massey' distinguished himself. (While these pages are in the press a brave warrior, 'Redan Massey,' Lord Clarina, has passed away). After a desperate hand-to-hand fight, those who were left alive of the forlorn hope were driven out. How it happened I leave others to say, but some of the wounded men were cursing and swearing at having been so shamefully deserted. No attempt was made to try a second attack, and the French were left to drive out the Russians single-handed.

I am simply relating what I saw with my own eyes, and I leave it to others to account for such a disgraceful proceeding.

I was frequently insulted afterwards by the French soldiers, who would shout in our faces, 'French *bon*, English no *bon*.'

I think I might mention here a little adventure I had one night in the trenches. We took down with us a small keg of rum, and during the night the sergeant and I went to serve out the rum to the men. I was sitting with the little keg between my knees, pouring out the rum into a tin held by a sergeant who knelt beside me. At that moment a large piece of shell smashed in the keg, and bulged the far side without coming out. 'Oh, the grog's all running away,' cried the sergeant; 'turn it round!'

Without dropping the keg, I turned it round and saved about half the liquor, but every man had only about half a glass; so, I sent up the broken keg immediately to the quartermaster in camp, with a polite request that we might have another, which in due course arrived, and the men had a full glass all round, so that they had altogether a glass and a half instead of one glass, to their great delight. I may mention that I was a total abstainer myself, and remained so during the whole campaign. It must have been rather a hot night, as we called it, for shortly after the second keg was emptied, something in the nature of a shot or splinter struck it, and one of the men shouted, 'You're too late, my boy; we've got it!' thus showing how reckless men get after a time. I have still got the piece of shell, weighing about 4 pounds, which struck the rum-keg as I held it.

One of the most abominable things we had to suffer in the trenches was a shower of iron bullets fired up in the air out of a mortar, and they came down perpendicularly, *whisk! whisk!* all around us, there being no protection from the parapet to save us.

I remember one night I found a man sitting next me quite dead; he had been killed by the iron shower.

Referring to the final attack: when I found that the British did not attempt to retake the redan, I quietly rode back to camp and had my dinner, returning again in the afternoon to see how matters were going on; but still there was no advance on our side, the battle between the French and the Russians raging furiously still.

The next morning, before daylight, I went down again, and rode through the trenches as far as our advanced sentries, where I met General Wyndham. Whether he had ever left the trenches I know not, but he took me kindly by the hand and said, 'Come, and I shall show you the redan.' I may say, therefore, I was the first in after the Russians had evacuated it; the killed on both sides, Russians and British, were lying just as they fell, and the general pointed out to me the whole scene, drawing my attention specially to one poor fellow lying at our feet. He said, 'Ah! that was a brave man; how splendidly he fought and rallied the others till he fell!' Seeing a Russian axe lying on the ground, I quietly hid it in a gabion amongst the loose earth, knowing that an order had been given that nothing was to be taken out of Sebastopol. I afterwards took off the handle and brought the head away, and have it now as one of my trophies.

The order above referred to was a most stupid one, for it did not extend to the French, who simply carried off everything that was valuable. For instance, I met six Frenchmen coming out with a magnificent grand piano on their heads, and everything that they fancied was taken out of the cathedral. One man came out with one of the splendid candlesticks from off the high altar, but on discovering in the daylight that it was not solid silver, he threw it down and kicked it to pieces. I picked up the base, which was all battered about, brought it home and had it restored, and it now stands on my sideboard.

When the embargo to looting was taken off, I took everything out of the town that I could make useful, but I had one most disagreeable duty to perform. I was ordered down with a large party to clear the Russian dead out of one of their hospitals, which had been left by them on their retreat, without making any effort for burial. The appearance of the place beggars all description. In a long room upstairs, which had evidently been a barrack, there was a row of beds on one side, in nearly every one of which there lay a corpse. One of the windows about the centre of the room stood wide open, and in the back court, just underneath, was a pile of human bodies, like an immense haystack, reaching nearly to the window.

Below this dreadful room there was a long passage dimly lighted, and all along, from one end to the other, lay the dead bodies of officers and soldiers. An immense pit had been excavated just in the rear of the redan, and into that we conveyed the sad remains by cartloads, and there they were all interred, and a great mound of earth heaped on the top of them. I was so fearfully nauseated that I could scarcely eat anything for three days, and appeared always to have a horrible taste in my mouth. This operation was all carried out within sight of the Russians, and in easy range of their guns from the other side of the harbour, where they were firmly established.

My principal duties were to bring up all necessaries supplied from Balaclava for the use of the division, and as the trenches were deserted, and as I now had plenty of spare transport—having amply supplied the needs of the commissariat for some time to come—I proceeded to establish myself and my men as comfortably as we could, seeing we had the prospect of another winter in the Crimea before us. One of our greatest troubles was the wandering away of the horses and mules from their picket-lines, so I started, with all the men I could muster, and built a wall about 4 feet high, forming the camp into a square, with an entrance off the high road to the front, and another to the rear, opening upon our parade-ground.

There was plenty of room all round, and we were not in any way crowded, and it was only about three minutes' smart walk to the 31st camp. The commissariat were on the other side of us, with a good space between. Outside my wall I dug a deep ditch and packed the soil against the wall on the outside, and no animal could pass either in or out. Then I started off with two waggons to the wood beyond the outposts of the Italians, who were encamped at the other end of the Balaclava plains, near where the memorable charge of the Light Brigade took place. On the way I picked up the lance-head of one of the 17th Lancers, and brought it home with me as a memento of that eventful day.

We spent a good many hours in felling and trimming trees, and were not disturbed by the Russians, although there was nothing to prevent them from taking us prisoners, had they known we were there.

With this timber I constructed two gates for my camp, also powerful picket-posts, to which I attached strong ropes taken out of Sebastopol. Then I had all my animals securely fastened, and there was no more trouble caused by their breaking loose.

We had to take them to water at a large pond within the French lines; but one fine morning I got the order to water them at the

Tchernaya River, some two miles away, as the pond was getting very low. I did not at all approve of this order, as the distance was so great; I therefore fell upon the following expedient: At the usual watering hour the halters were all taken off, and the horses and mules were driven out at the open gate. Away they went, kicking and squealing with delight, right away to the pond for their drink, plunging in and setting the French sentries at defiance. The moment they had left their own camp their corn was put down in a little heap for each animal; and by that device they soon came back again for their dinner, and were tied up without any trouble. No complaint was ever lodged by the French, and I continued to carry out this wise and common-sense plan, until a plentiful rain filled up the pond, and official permission was given for the use of it, as formerly.

Having plenty of spare waggons and the hearty permission of the divisional staff, I went down daily to Sebastopol, with a party of men, and we brought up from there every conceivable article that might be useful for a standing camp, ripping off the floors of the houses and bringing up plenty of wood, besides nails of all sorts, a barrel of tar, a quantity of ship's sails, lots of iron to make horseshoes, and last, but not least, a fine big grindstone.

The general sent me a lot of efficient workmen, picked out from the different regiments—shoeing-smiths, carpenters, bricklayers, etc. I set to work at once and put up stables for all the transport, and to build a comfortable house for myself, which I did out of the Sebastopol stones, with the funnel of a small steamboat for my chimney; I built a fireplace and a partition-wall to make two rooms with English firebricks; and there was no trouble in making a grate with some old iron. As we were awfully tormented by this time with armies of rats, I filled the whole of the space under the floor with smashed empty bottles, so that never a rat attempted to come in. The doors and windows I dug out of a house in Sebastopol, so that they had only to be built in frames and all, without any alteration. They were beautiful mahogany doors, with brass fittings—one for the entrance and the other leading to the bedroom. The partition was built so as to leave half of the funnel in each room, and a log or two on the fire, when I went to bed, kept both rooms warm all night.

Then I put a lean-to against each side of the house—one was for my servant, Joe Brown, and the other was my office. I also had a boiler fixed in Joe's room by an efficient bricklayer who knew his work, and a little fire-place for cooking; and I could always have enough hot water to warm my bath all through the winter, the bath being a fine large tub I brought out of Sebastopol. One of the bandsmen of the 31st papered my rooms with a pretty rose-bud pattern which I purchased in Balaclava. The roof was composed of planks, neatly fitted together without any overlap and then covered with strong canvas taken from the dockyard, nailed carefully on with copper nails, and then well tarred. I believe that my house was the very best to be seen in either of the armies, and many a happy evening my friend and I had together, as I had a carpet and beautiful tables and chairs out of Sebastopol.

I spent a very pleasant autumn and winter until peace was declared, when we made up parties of officers and proceeded to explore the country in all directions. Our first trip was to the battlefield of the Alma, as it was announced in general orders that on a certain date the country was thrown open to us by the Russians. Being determined to be first, we sat up till twelve o'clock at night, and then started on horseback with two days' food for ourselves and horses in our saddle-bags, but no attendants. I was selected to be guide, and after crossing the Tchernaya by the bridge, I took a beeline for the Alma, although I had never been there in my life, but knew the direction by the map.

There was no road, but we simply climbed hills and rode through woods, getting there all right. We first rode up the hill which the French had so gallantly taken from the Russians, and found on the top the skeletons of six horses, lying two and two, with the remains of the harness still lying there—evidently the spot where the French had captured the guns, and had shot the horses as they stood, to prevent the enemy from taking them away. I brought home with me one of the horses' feet with the Russian brand on it, and have it now. The shoe is still on it.

After wandering about for some time, we took possession of a hut without a roof, lighted a fire, and made ourselves as comfortable as circumstances permitted, including the horses; had a sound sleep, taking by turns to watch our horses all night, as there were Cossacks about; but they were quite friendly, and invited us to come to their quarters, which we politely declined, and returned to Sebastopol in the morning.

A day or two after this, I saw an open carriage with two ladies inside passing my camp. I went down, making myself as pleasant as I could, and asked them in Italian if I could be of any service to them. They replied in fluent Italian, though they were Russians, that they would be grateful if I would show them about. Needless to add, I complied at once with their request, while the coachman and horses were taken charge of by my men. I introduced them to my great friend Dr. Atkinson, of the 31st, and after wandering about for some time, we four returned to my house, and had lunch. One of the ladies informed us that she was in Sebastopol when the Allies arrived outside, and that they had nothing to do then but walk in. Oh, if they had only known this! Those in Sebastopol were very much surprised when no effort was made to take possession of the city, seeing the Russian Army was absent!

After lunch, with many polite thanks, the ladies requested their carriage might be brought round. Fancy my feelings when I went out to give orders, to find the coachman quite drunk and utterly helpless! After spending a very enjoyable evening all together, and having introduced the ladies to several of my brother officers who could talk Italian, I handed over my house to the unexpected visitors, and got a shakedown for myself in the 31st camp. I lodged the coachman safe in the guard-room, with strict orders that he was on no account to get another drop of liquor, and am happy to add that he was quite capable in the morning to return home to a Russian town some eighteen miles off.

Having very little to do, we spent most of our time making expeditions all round the country. Dr. Atkinson and I started one morning for an expedition in the direction of Batchybacserai.

We generally hunted up an hotel where we had a dinner for which the Russians charged a fabulous sum, and then rode quietly home again in the evening.

On this occasion we stayed rather later than usual, and it was dark when we started our ride home. As the town stood some two miles at right angles to the road, I suggested that we should make a short cut until we struck the main road. It was a very dark night, and after we had ridden some time, I saw what I took to be a man carrying a lantern some distance in front of us, so I trotted forward. As soon as I began to near the man, he ran away as fast as I could trot. I then put the horse into a gallop, and still he kept just as far as ever in front. I was going after him as fast as I could pelt, when my companion shouted out, 'For goodness' sake, stop!' and I pulled up short. He said, 'That is not a man at all, but a will-o'-the-wisp, and I am certain he is leading you into danger.'

And sure enough, within 20 yards of where I had pulled up, we came upon a long row of deep pits which had been a Russian camp in the former winter. The Russians had dug right down a deep square pit into the ground, and roofed it over, very much as the inhabitants used to do on the other side of the Rocky Mountains. In this case the roofs had entirely disappeared; no doubt they had been used for firewood. I had a very narrow escape.

Whatever people may think of this, I have simply stated the facts. No man could have possibly run as fast as I was galloping.

Shortly after this we struck the main road and got quietly back to camp.

Our next expedition was to visit Simferopol. As it was some fifty miles away, we had to make arrangements accordingly. We took an Irish outside car and harnessed four horses to it. Then we filled the well of the car right up with oats for the horses, started with two postilions, and did the journey in first-rate style.

When we got to Simferopol, we found all the hotels crammed full, not a bed to be had for love or money, but as a favour one of the hotel-keepers gave me the use of a sofa in the dining-room. After dinner I retired for the night on to the sofa, but to my great astonishment a large table was spread for a fresh party of diners, and in came some half-dozen Englishmen and Russians. I understood from the conversation that the Englishmen were going to stand the dinner. Only one of the Russians spoke English; and it was really past a joke, after champagne had been going round for some time, all the English shouting at once, 'Tell him, tell him!'

This abominable row went on, to my great annoyance, till daylight in the morning. By that time, they had got rid of a good stock of champagne, and when they cleared out, I had some chance of going to sleep; but my revenge was sweet when the bill came in to the Englishmen in the morning after the Russians had departed. I heard one item repeated several times—'Twenty bottles of champagne, twenty sovereigns,' so my noisy friends had to pay for their amusement.

Having seen all that we cared to see there, we trotted quietly home again,

This time Atkinson, his cousin, and Swettenham (my former subaltern in the 31st, and later a general) made up the party. We had started on the Woronzoff Road, intending to take a trip all along that lovely belt of narrow land which extends nearly the whole length of the southern face of the Crimea, protected from the north for many miles by high and impassable cliffs.

The entrance to this was by a high and lofty gateway, standing on the top of the cliff, and in no other way could you get down to this beautiful strip of country, where olive-trees and vines flourished in quite a tropical climate, and the wild flowers were most lovely.

The first night we stopped at an hotel, where we were very well received, and the next day we arrived at Livadia, the winter palace of the *Czar*. It is well known that the Allies left this beautiful place quite intact, and nothing could have been easier than to blow it all to pieces by a single man-of-war, as it stood on the seashore.

We were most politely received and escorted all over the palace (which was in perfect order) by a gentleman who walked backwards the whole way, and appeared incapable of walking like other human beings, from long practice!

After this we did another long day's march, but I am sorry to say that I forget the name of the place at which we stopped that night, and then returned as we came.

We were certainly in light marching order, and carried no extras, but we were quite used to roughing it in those days, and everyone knows that the lighter a horse is for a long journey the better.

The weather being now delightfully warm, we used to make up parties to go down and swim in Sebastopol Harbour, and occasionally I used to march the men down to the Tchernaya River.

On one such occasion we found the river in flood, and coming down in rather a muddy condition. While the men were plunging about, I and the doctor walked up and down about 50 yards off.

Suddenly we heard some of the men calling out, 'There he is, there he is!' in an excited manner, and I saw them pointing at the river. I realised in a moment that there was something wrong. I was dressed in uniform, with my sword and a pair of high Life-Guard boots and spurs. In a moment I unbuckled my sword and dropped it, knocked my cap off, and ran forward as fast as I could. Just as I got within 10 yards of the river, where there was a perpendicular bank about 5 feet high and a deep whirling pool, a shout came from all the men, 'There he is again!' and as I came in sight of the water I saw a black head disappear. Without checking my steps, I mentally calculated the distance, took a header into the river, and grappled with the man at the bottom, and brought him safe out, but too far gone to struggle.

The extraordinary thing was that with all those men on the bank, some of whom were expert swimmers, not one of them attempted to save their comrade; but after I got hold of him, Sergeant Connelly, my quartermaster sergeant, jumped in and helped me to fish him out.

I handed him over to the doctor, got on my horse, and rode home to get a change of clothes.

This little exploit of mine appeared in *The Times*, in one of Russell's letters home, but without any particulars.

The following anecdote is about a scene before the Peace:

About the time I began to build my house, I was one afternoon improving the entrance to the camp, and happened to be looking in the direction of the French lines, when I saw one of the grandest sights that can possibly be imagined—to wit, the blowing up of an old windmill, in which the French had an enormous quantity of live shells. The walls acted exactly like a cone, and when the explosion occurred, a stream of fire shot straight up into the air, immediately forming into an immense white head, out of which exploded hundreds of live shells, the splinters coming down again in a perfect shower, making the ground all round dance with little jets of dust.

The whole French Army turned out on the spot, as they seemed to anticipate an attack, and at the moment, I suppose, they did not know what had happened. The bursting of the shells sounded like the discharge of artillery, and no doubt, for the moment, they thought that the Russians had stolen a march on them.

I should like to record the faithful service of a Jew, given while in the Crimea, where, by his request, I took him. He was a native of Zante, by trade a tailor, and an uncommonly good one, too, Raphael Levi by name. On one of my trips in the *Lizzie* to Corfu, Raphael came on board and told me that, on account of the evil treatment which the Jews received from the Greeks, he had been actually refused his passage on the usual steamer back to Zante. It can scarcely be believed how the Jews were persecuted, the more particularly on account of their belief in the British, while the Greeks were rabidly Russian, and it was the desire to prevent complications that caused the British garrison not at once to be sent to the Crimea.

Levi said that if I would only take him back with me, he would provide all his own food, and would only ask to be allowed to sleep on deck. Of course, I took him, and when he came on board next morning, accompanied by some friends, he told me that for my kindness there was not a Jew in Corfu who would not be my friend in the future. Later on, when we received orders to embark for the Crimea, Levi asked to be allowed to come as my servant, and knowing what a useful man he was, I accepted his offer, and he came on board, living amongst my own men, who knew him and liked him, so that there was no trouble on that account during the passage.

On arrival I found him invaluable, as there were a number of his own people there, and anything that was to be got he managed to obtain for us.

I may just mention one little incident:

In the depth of winter one of my officers was taken dangerously ill with quinsy, and the doctor declared that it was absolutely necessary to apply leeches to save his life.

The thermometer was below zero, and it was blowing a wild blizzard with drifting snow. Levi said that it was just possible that leeches might be got from some of his people beyond the French lines several miles away. He volunteered to go for them if I would give him a horse, rolled himself up as well as he could, and started. After some two or three hours he returned, more dead than alive, but announced that he had at last got leeches. Then with the greatest difficulty unbuttoning one coat after another, he produced the bottle from his chest. Fancy our astonishment when we found the bottle frozen solid!

The doctor took the matter in hand, thawed out the leeches skilfully, and they did their duty. I call that an act of heroism on the part of Levi.

By-and-by Levi got permission to start a canteen and a sort of shop; he made a very good thing out of it, I should hope.

My battalion of transport was left to nearly the last when the army embarked for England.

We had no horses, and had nothing to do, so we devoted ourselves principally to rat-hunting, as the brutes perfectly swarmed about the camps, because they were starving.

One night one of the men came home drunk, and went to sleep in an empty stable. His remains were found in the morning half eaten; whether the rats ate him alive or not will never be known.

Our last amusement was to collect the huts from all the neighbouring camps and pile them up in an enormous heap on the ground. When the evening began to close in, we set fire to it. It was the biggest bonfire I fancy that ever was seen. Some of the men took a circular platform from a tent, made a table of it at the highest point of the pile, put chairs round, and had it well supplied with bottles full of powder.

To make the affair still more comical, several human-like figures were manufactured with old clothes and straw; some of them had a bottle of powder inside. They were tied to the chairs and set round the table. The fun was, of course, to see them blow up when they took fire.

Everyone that went up into the air was received with a loud cheer, but by-and-by the fire became so fierce that no one could go within 100 yards of it, and it burned for days. My last act was to set fire to my own beautiful house, plastered and papered inside, with wooden floors and mahogany doors with brass mountings—the whole, as I have already related, brought from the town.

It is not surprising that shipowners made a good thing out of it at this time. The steamer that we came home in, the *Robert Low*, being chartered by the day or week, was in no hurry to arrive in England. I calculated afterwards by the time that we were on the passage, and the distance from Balaclava to Portsmouth, that we did it exactly at two and a half miles an hour, but we enjoyed it thoroughly, stopping at every conceivable place on the way home, and often spending a few days on shore. First Constantinople, then Malta, Gibraltar, and Lisbon, where we had a most enjoyable week; then Falmouth, and ultimately, we arrived safely at Portsmouth.

Off Cowes we steamed past the royal yacht at anchor. Her Majesty was sitting on deck in an armchair. She gracefully bowed to us as we gave her three ringing cheers.

CHAPTER 11

Outbreak of the Indian Mutiny

It was now decided by the government to establish a Military Train on the same lines as that of the French.

The land-transport of about fourteen battalions, commanded by various officers, was disbanded, and out of the four commanding officers, only two were selected for the new corps. Major Salis—a fine old veteran from the Cape Mounted Rifles—and myself were the two selected; all the other officers were either sent back to their regiments or put on half-pay. I was sent off to the different cavalry regiments stationed in England or Ireland, to select volunteers for the new corps, and my orders were to take none but those of really good character. I created a tremendous disturbance by rejecting about half of the offered volunteers, and strong remonstrances were sent to headquarters by the different commanding officers; but the Horse Guards approved of my proceedings, and I got together 500 as fine young men as could be seen anywhere.

We were then sent to the Curragh Camp in Ireland to organize and get in good order. Within a very few months an economic fit seized the authorities, and I got orders to divide the regiment in two, and send half over to England to form the 6th Battalion, mine being the 2nd. Of course, I selected the best, both of non-commissioned officers and men, and had as fine a body of men as was ever collected together in one regiment. Many of my sergeants were old non-commissioned officers from the Life Guards, Scots Greys, and Light Cavalry regiments; also, some Horse Artillerymen.

In the early spring war broke out with China in 1856, and our commandant, Colonel McMurdo, was ordered to detail the most efficient battalion for foreign service, and mine, the 2nd Battalion, had the honour of being selected. Levi (now our master tailor), who was

144

a universal favourite, wanted to go with us and offered to enlist, but, notwithstanding his high qualifications, his age was against him. The authorities refused to let him join, and sent us in his place a miserable little wretch who had never been on a horse in his life, and refused point-blank to mount anything. He actually walked all through the Indian Mutiny, in which we were afterwards engaged, and, of course, was never in action. He was looked upon as part of the baggage.

Levi came to see us off when we embarked at Woolwich. The tears were running down his cheeks as he said goodbye. I heard afterwards that he had gone to Alexandria, and was doing well, but I never saw him again, although ever since I have had a warm corner in my heart for the Jews.

The voyage was uneventful, and as we had no ladies on board, we had no rows.

When we arrived at the Straits of Sunda, we had to anchor three times on account of a foul wind, and each time had to put back again. On the third occasion we landed and called upon the British Consul, and heard, to our great astonishment, of the terrible Mutiny in India. Things were at their worst there, and so he had orders to divert the whole of the squadron sailing for China to Calcutta.

The captain of the ship was furious at being diverted to Calcutta, as he had a nice little private spec on board to sell at Hong Kong. This, of course, we did not know at the time. He refused to go unless I gave him a written order, after having done his best to frighten me by telling me of the fearful risks I was running by breaking the ship's charter and altering the ship's destination. However, I stuck to my point, and to Calcutta he had to go.

On arrival at Calcutta I proceeded at once to report myself to Sir Colin Campbell, the commander-in-chief, who was then staying at Government House with Lord Canning.

My interview with him was delightfully characteristic of the man.

His first question was, 'What are you, and what can you do?'

I replied, 'We can do anything.'

'Anything!' he cried, in violent excitement; 'what do you mean?'

'Sir,' I answered, 'we can act as infantry or cavalry, or drive artillery guns; but we are not gunners, though my men can all ride and drive a pair.'

'What do you mean,' he said, 'by saying you can do cavalry?'

'Why,' I replied, 'we are nearly all trained cavalrymen, and we can act as such.'

'Take care what you say, young man; remember, if I make you cavalry and you fail, the responsibility will fall on me, not you.' And then in a very sharp voice he asked, 'Are you prepared to take that responsibility?'

I said, 'I am, sir.'

Without another word he seized me by the collar as if I had been a schoolboy, saying, 'Come along with me;' and he trotted me down a long passage and knocked at a door. An *aide-de-camp* opened, and Sir Colin said, 'Can I see Lord Canning?'

'I'll see, Sir Colin.' *the aide-de-camp* replied, and we sat down in the ante-room.

Almost immediately we were shown into the governor-general's private room. I can see him now, sitting at a desk covered with papers, with a pen in his hand. He had a handsome face, but was pale and careworn.

Sir Colin at once said: 'My lord, here's an officer just arrived with 250 men, and he says he can turn them into a cavalry regiment. Have you any cavalry horses?'

'Yes,' replied His Excellency; 'we have 500 eating their heads off in the *coolie* bazaar, belonging to such and such a native regiment, which we have had to dismount as being untrustworthy at the present juncture. You have my authority to take as many of them as you require to mount the regiment.'

So ended my interview.

It will be seen from the foregoing that I had a private interview with the two greatest men in India, and that they had assumed the responsibility of converting us into a cavalry regiment. Of course, as they had taken this responsibility on my word, I was bound to do everything in my power to make it a success, and we were watched with the greatest interest by Sir Colin Campbell throughout the whole of our career in India.

Sir Colin afterwards asked me what equipment I required. I told him everything but carbines, as we had no saddlery or equipment of any kind. 'Let me have a list,' he said, 'of everything.' The list was made out the next day on half a sheet of foolscap, and not even in duplicate, and was complied with at once—red-tape was evidently dead and buried here for the present crisis, quires of paper and weeks of delay would have been the order of the day before we could have got a single article at home.

The next day we disembarked and marched into Fort William,

where we were quartered for a few weeks. We were to start up-country with the first force got together.

All this happened so many years ago that it may be interesting to know how we proceeded to get ready for active service half a century back. The regiment consisted of four troops, and early in the morning and within forty-eight hours of the foregoing conversation with the commander-in-chief, I took the four officers commanding the troops, with their sergeant-majors, down to the horses, which were picketed in the open 500 well-bred Arabs, thoroughly and perfectly free from vice, which is a characteristic of Arab horses. To the senior officer I said, 'What colour will you have?'

He answered, 'Chestnuts.'

The next chose 'greys,' the third 'bay,' and number four had to take a mixed lot. The officers and their sergeant-majors then proceeded to select their horses, and, as fast as they did so, they were taken away and picketed by themselves in four lines. They were then branded by our farriers in the front of the hoof with a number and the letter of the troop, A, B, C, or D, as the case might be, these being the troop letters.

Next morning the regiment was marched down, every man with his saddle on his head and his bridle in his hand, and each selected his own horse. Some took horses that at all events looked quiet; others selected high-spirited looking animals—every man according to his taste, the sergeants, of course, having the first picking. After each man had chosen his horse he stood at its head, and as soon as the selection was over, we mounted and rode down to the Ganges to water the horses, and it turned out a splendid success, as they were beautifully trained and everything that could be wished. They soon took to their new masters.

Sir Colin inspected us after a few days, and we were almost immediately ordered to march upcountry with a force of all arms, under the Hon. Colonel Berkeley.

The first amusing incident occurred as we marched out of the fort:

A volunteer guard turned out to do us honour. They were the most miserable set of creatures you could imagine. Of course, their muskets were all loaded, and just as I was opposite the guard their commanding officer gave the order, 'Present arms!' Every man's musket went up to his shoulder, and was levelled right at my head, with their fingers on the trigger. 'No, no!' screamed the officer in command; 'it's the other "present!"' And, fortunately, without a single musket going off, they held them all up in the air.

147

I may here mention that the King of Oude was a prisoner in Fort William, and when I was field officer for the day my duty was to visit His Majesty in bed during the night to shake him, so as to see that he was not a pillow dressed up. So soon as he gave a grunt, then I felt satisfied, and retired.

We were for some time quartered at Dum-Dum while Colonel Berkeley's little force was being got together. Here we had stabling for our horses, which was much more convenient than having to march down to the *Coolie* bazaar for it. My first charger was a splendid chestnut, sixteen hands high. He had probably never been in a stable in his life before, and in getting up he slipped his hind-legs and dislocated his stifle-joint—the only time I have ever seen such an accident. The result was that he walked with his hind-leg straight out behind him without being able to move it. By seizing him by the head and pushing him violently backwards the joint used to go in again with a snap; but this was rather a dangerous horse to ride on service, and so I sent him back to the ranks, and selected a grey.

I think I may mention here what I consider was a rather remarkable occurrence—*i.e.*, that on both of these horses during the Mutiny an officer was killed. Lieutenant Dawson was shot off the chestnut, and Captain Nason, who joined the regiment after I was invalided, and took over my horse and camp equipment, was shot off the grey.

We duly arrived at Allahabad without falling in with any of the enemy so far.

On the way up we had two rivers to cross; the first, I am sorry to say, I forget the name of, but it was rather a small one which could be forded without difficulty. We were told there were some dangerous quicksands in the bed of the river, so I went down in a pair of pyjamas and flannel shirt and waded up and down, and backwards and forwards, in the water, until I discovered what I considered a good safe crossing-place, marking it with a pole on each bank, and we availed ourselves of it the next morning.

The other river was the well-known one called the Sone, and after a long day's march we were sent forward a second march after dark to discover the ford here also, and I was told that a guide would meet us when we got to the banks of the river. We were very sleepy and tired. I nearly fell asleep on my horse, and I had to trot the regiment to keep them awake. When we got to the bank of the river, which was a wide expanse of sand, no guide was to be seen, and we had the place all to ourselves. It would have been folly to have attempted to ford the river

148

in the dark; besides, I had to ascertain exactly where the ford was, so I dismounted the regiment. Every man slipped his arm through his bridle, and lay down beside his horse. Having posted a picket, I followed the men's example and lay down also, and soon fell fast asleep. When I awoke in the morning daylight was just coming in. I got up and shook myself, and saw the most remarkable and extraordinary sight that ever was seen. Every man and every horse was lying down stretched on the sand apparently dead-beat, and still fast asleep; some of the men's legs were over the horses' backs or necks, and some of the horses were resting their heads on their riders.

We shook ourselves together, and waiting until the commanding officer and the rest came up, we got safely across the river, and proceeded on the march.

We were overtaken at Allahabad by the commander-in-chief, who had now got a strong army together, and we then marched in the direction of Cawnpore.

We crossed the Ganges by a bridge of boats, and so on to Lucknow, to relieve the garrison under Sir Henry Havelock and General Outram, whose brilliant defences and whose fearful hardships are all a matter of history (see Captain Trotter's *Life of Outram*).

When halted at Lucknow I went to visit that awful well at Cawnpore in which were buried the women and children who had been slaughtered by Nana Sahib, and afterwards out to the encampment where a brave handful of men gallantly defended themselves from the constant attacks of the dastardly Nana Sahib, until they were, unfortunately, persuaded to move on a promise of safe conduct. This also is a matter of history, and on it I need not dwell.

The whole of the betrayed party had been in some old barracks without roofs. There was therefore nothing to burn, fortunately, and we wandered through the dilapidated rooms. Every here and there we came upon holes right through where cannon-shot had passed. A little bit of paper, fastened on with a piece of wood, beside one of these holes had on it, written in a lady's hand, 'It was here that Mrs. So-and-so was killed on such a date,' and I took up a little baby's pink slipper, which I brought away as a remembrance. You have no idea of the feeling of anger that these sights aroused in the breasts of every man in the force. We were ready to cut down mercilessly almost every man that we met.

Before going further, I ought to mention the officers under my command. Captain Wyatt was my senior captain, an able and experienced officer, who had passed some years of his life in Ceylon, and was well known as a good elephant shot. He was posted to the 2nd Battalion after we were under orders for active service, and got leave of absence from the Horse Guards till the day of embarkation.

I happened to be at the Horse Guards on some little matter of business, as I had plenty of friends there, when the Duke of Cambridge (commander in-chief) passed through the room, on his way to his own apartment. In a minute or two I had a message to go and see His Royal Highness. When I went in he proceeded to ask me a number of questions about the regiment, and also pointed out that, this being our first duty since we had been raised, and as I had been specially selected to go, he expected that we should do our duty well; and as we were a newly-raised corps, he trusted that we would conduct ourselves to his entire satisfaction.

He then asked about the officers, and I said that they were very satisfactory, but that the senior captain had never joined the regiment, and had leave until embarkation. Without a word His Royal Highness rang the bell and said, 'I wish to see the adjutant-general and quartermaster-general.' Almost immediately both of these gentlemen walked in. The adjutant-general was General Wetherall, well known for his very short temper.

The duke said, 'Major Robertson informs me that Captain Wyatt, the senior captain, has never joined the regiment, and has got leave until embarkation. Please order him to join at once. Good-morning.'

I could see that the adjutant-general was, to say the least of it, excited as he retired, and when I left the duke a few minutes afterwards, I found him waiting for me at the end of the passage. He rushed at me with his fist clenched and raised in the air, and literally screamed out, 'You dare to report me to the commander-in-chief!' Then shook both his fists in my face, and turned round and dashed into his room, shutting the door with a slam which shook the whole of the house.

An old door-keeper who was standing a few yards off with his arms up in the air exclaimed, 'Oh dear, oh dear! I never did see the old gentleman so high in his stirrups before.'

So much for my first introduction to Captain Wyatt. He went through the whole of the Mutiny, and, after I was invalided, commanded the regiment with success and distinction, for which he was promoted to major and C.B.; and when the corps was disbanded, he got an appointment from Lord Penrhyn in North Wales, having charge of his extensive estates. He was succeeded at his death by Mr.

Chevenix Trench, a nephew of the celebrated Archbishop Chevenix Trench of Dublin, well known as Dean of Westminster for many years. Wyatt's books are standard for army examinations to this day.

The next officer that I come to, and who commanded my first squadron, was Captain Godfrey Clerk, son of Sir George Russell Clerk, K.C.B., G.C.S.I., Governor of Bombay in the year 1848, and previously referred to in this volume as political officer when the 31st went to take the fort of Kytul. Later on, Sir George filled other important posts in the Indian Government.

I must mention here that Captain Clerk was commanding a troop of my regiment, and was a squadron leader. He was a splendid officer—the best I had—and although an infantry officer, like myself he was a first-rate rider, and in a very short time quite at home in the command of a troop of cavalry.

At the advance on Lucknow, he, with a squadron of our mounted infantry, led the advance of the army to that city, together with the 16th Lancers.

During one of the charges they had to cross an ugly ditch. Not a single man of Clerk's squadron fell, though, owing to the difficulty of negotiating it, several of the lancers came bad croppers.

Captain Clerk, when telling me of the incident, showed natural pride in his men's horsemanship; and I am glad to narrate the above, which not only shows what a picked set my men were, but which may interest my old comrade should it meet his eye, when he will be able to corroborate it. Clerk had attached to his squadron an officer of the Bays, who, poor fellow, was killed in the same charge where Dr. McArthur also was so badly wounded.

But this is an old story. Captain Clerk is now, (1906), a general and an extra equerry to the king. May he long be spared to fill an honourable and useful life!

My third captain was Captain Inglefield, brother to the well-known Arctic explorer, Admiral Inglefield. He, poor fellow, was not very strong, but willing and active. He succumbed to the fatigues of the campaign.

My fourth troop commander was Lieutenant B——, as I shall call him.

I decline to give his name, as I wish to record an event which occurred shortly before we went into action. One morning I found upon the table in my tent a sheet of paper with a round-robin, and the signatures of the whole troop surrounding it in such a way that the list had neither beginning nor end. Underneath were these words, 'We, the above-signed, refuse to go into action under command of Lieutenant B——, as we have no confidence in his leadership.' I need not say that this document was not made public by me, as it would have been a fearful slur upon the regiment; but after consultation with the adjutant, I quietly transferred another officer to the command of the troop. As may be supposed, Lieutenant B—— did not distinguish himself throughout the campaign.

I had several first-rate officers who had been raised from the ranks; and my adjutant, Lieutenant Devine, was an old horse artilleryman, and thereby quite at home with horses and harness, and admirably suited for the appointment, which he held for many years.

I shall have occasion to refer to our doctor, McArthur, further on.

One of my subalterns could almost have been called a 'wild Irishman,' so impetuous was he, and on every occasion distinguished himself by his reckless bravery. He belonged to the old family of the Bodkins of the North of Ireland.

So, on the whole, I may say we were very well provided, although there was not a single cavalry officer amongst us.

My first squadron, under Captain Clerk, had the honour of being in the advance-guard along with the 16th Lancers, while I, with the other squadron, composed the rear-guard. I remember going to the commander-in-chief and asking him to be allowed to join the advance-guard instead of the rear. He politely informed me that he wanted an officer in the rear whom he could depend on, so I had not another word to say. We marched all day, and towards evening my rearguard was attacked by a lot of infantry skirmishers, who were amongst the mango groves outside Lucknow.

I dismounted a troop, and with their carbines we soon drove them back. We got no orders all day, and we simply followed the regiment in front of us. When it became quite dark, we halted. Every man put his arm through his horse's bridle, lay down just where he was, and we were soon all fast asleep. My dismounted men were placed as a small picket in the rear.

I had several dismounted men, owing to their horses having sore backs, and I posted them in our rear as a picket. We were terribly bothered by sore backs during the whole campaign, and my saddlers were everlastingly padding the saddles to protect the horses' withers; but the unfortunate thing was that the saddle-trees were so badly made that they opened out with the weight of the men, and a saddle that fitted a horse perfectly in the morning might be sawing his withers before night. These saddles, I need not say, had all been made in India. I may just mention that the colonel of the Madras Regiment, whose saddles we obtained in Calcutta, had an allowance for saddlery, and no doubt made a good thing of it.

On awakening in the morning just at daylight, I looked up and saw sentries of the 93rd Highlanders in full costume on our left. It must be understood that the army was circling round Lucknow to attack from the other side, and we, the cavalry, and some of the artillery, were stationed at the palace of Dilkusha in charge of the commissariat and reserve ammunition. Colonel Little of the 16th Lancers was in command, and I was second.

For some days the infantry had desperate hand-to-hand fighting through the town until they penetrated to the Residency.

In the meantime, we had constant skirmishes with parties of the enemy's infantry, who, however, were easily driven off with very little loss on our side.

One evening as I was posting the vedettes to the rear of the camp, the ground being all more or less wooded and enclosed by a high wall as it was a royal park, I saw a fine stag about 50 yards off standing looking at me. I said to Jones, for that was the old man's name whom I had just posted (he was afterwards wheeler-sergeant for many years), 'Hand me your carbine.' I took a steady aim, hit the stag fair in the forehead, and dropped him in his tracks. He made a grand addition to the mess dinner for some days.

A little further round, the same night, when close to the west side of the park, we saw a party of our grass-cutters hotly pursued by some of the enemy. In a moment we dismounted, seized our carbines, and ran out into the open to meet them. One volley sent the enemy scampering back faster than they came, and our grass-cutters got safe into camp with their loads on their heads. It said much for their pluck that, when hotly pursued and fired at, not one of them dropped his bundle of grass.

One morning word came to Colonel Little that a company of Sikhs who had been left in Bank's Bungalow (as the house was called) were cut off from the rest of the army, and were starving. The road passed straight down into Lucknow from our camp, but there was a wide canal separating us from the town. There was a difficulty in reaching the Sikhs, the bridge having been blown away, and there was only a fragment of the central pier standing above water.

DILKUSHA, 1857

When we got down to where the bridge had been, two Sikhs were waiting us on the other side. We had brought with us several small sacks of flour and a good supply of rope; but the distance across was so great that our utmost efforts could not make the rope reach the other side, and Colonel Little reluctantly said, 'I'm afraid we can do nothing for the poor fellows.'

I said, 'I think I can manage it.' So, I pulled off my coat, sword, and boots, and walked down to the bank of the canal. Just as I went into the water a horrid little water-snake began to spit at me, but I splashed the water into his face till he took himself off. I then swam off to the pier in the middle of the bridge, and having previously made arrangements that they should tie a sack in the centre of the long rope, the men on our bank threw me down the end of the rope. As soon as I got it, they lowered the sack, and I pulled hard and landed it safely on the fragment of pier showing above the water. There was just room for the sack, but none for me, so I had to remain in the water.

Once the sack rested securely on the pier, the other end of the rope was then thrown down to me. I coiled it up and threw it, and the first shot landed it safe in the hands of the Sikhs. Then, holding on tight to my half of the rope, I let out as they hauled in and the sack was happily landed quite dry on their side. This operation was performed three or four times, till all the sacks were got safely over.

I then swam back, jumped on my horse, and galloped back to camp as hard as I could, for the water had been very cold.

I caused considerable excitement in camp, riding in dripping wet and half dressed; but I soon changed my clothes, and was none the worse. I received a most grateful message of thanks from the Sikhs and their officer for what I had done.

The Residency, as history relates, was relieved. One evening, a day or two after, I met Sir Henry Havelock, all alone, walking quietly towards our camp. He looked very pale and careworn, and was walking very slowly. I was greatly shocked and unprepared for the news that the tremendous *mental* strain which he had undergone had been too much for him, for he was entirely above *bodily* fear, and was one of those brave heroes who adorn the history of our country. He did his work nobly, and he lay down and died a few hours after I had seen him.

He was buried quietly in the garden of the Alum Bagh, and every commanding officer in the army attended his funeral. The same evening that I met Sir Henry walking I saw a party of the rescued women. I was much amused at their costumes. I got it on the very best authority afterwards that they were so loaded with plundered jewellery and gold ornaments, which they had sown inside their petticoats, that it was with difficulty that some of them were able to walk.

I gave up the use of my tent to a party of them, and the kind return they made for it was helping themselves to (I will not say stealing) my only teapot—an article not at all plentiful in Lucknow.

One afternoon, while riding about by myself, and keeping my eyes wide open, as I was on neutral ground—between Dilkusha and the fighting in the city—I saw a *doolie*, evidently occupied, wandering about in a very uncertain fashion, as the bearers had apparently lost their way. I rode up to it, and to my great surprise found Sir Archibald Alison inside, with one arm badly shattered. He was in imminent danger of being cut off by the enemy, so I escorted the *doolie* back with me, and saw him safely lodged in hospital, where I believe his arm was amputated.

A night or two after this an escort arrived at the Dilkusha Palace in charge of the King of Oude's brother and a young princess; I am not sure whether she was a daughter or a niece. They were handed over to me with strict orders for their safe custody, so I requested His Royal Highness to step into an empty room in the basement of the palace, and on this the young lady raised a fearful outcry of, '*Hum ne jaga, hum ne jaga!*' meaning 'I won't go!' and His Royal Highness declined also, so I helped him in with the tip of my boot, and carried the lady in my arms, placing two sentries at the door.

In one of the charges made by the advance-guard when approaching Lucknow, our doctor, McArthur, had to ride with the rest of Clerk's squadron, as he could not possibly stay behind, and he was hit in the back of the neck with a splinter of shell. This must in some way have touched his spine and affected his brain, for he became wildly insane and, being an Irishman, developed a strong wish to fight or kill somebody. We had no means of confining him, and some of the officers had taken charge of him, but he was so dangerous that they were glad to get rid of him. Ultimately, I took him into my tent, a small one, 12 feet square, and I shall never forget the result as long as I live.

My sword, which had been well sharpened by a professional Sikh, was hanging to the tent-pole, and my revolver opposite it, in its belt. McArthur's bed was on one side of the tent, and mine was on the opposite side. As soon as he got into bed, he shouted to his servant to bring him a light for his pipe. The man brought in a piece of red-hot charcoal and put it on the top of the pipe. The doctor immediately

156

covered himself all over, head and all, and proceeded to pull at the pipe as hard as he could, the smoke coming out all round from under the blankets (for the weather being very cold we had to keep ourselves warm). In an incredibly short time, the pipe was finished and he asked for another, which he smoked in the same manner. Then he jumped out of bed, seized my sword, and drawing it, rushed out of the tent, shouting, 'I hear them, I hear them! I will kill them! I will teach them to call me a coward.'

Following him, I ran out, caught him, and said: 'You give me the sword and I will kill them for you.'

Two or three times he went through the same performance, till I fell asleep. How long I slept I know not, but when I awoke the tent was pitch dark, while a terrible weight was upon my chest, and there was the maniac sitting upon me, while he hissed into my ear: 'You were my last friend, and now you have deserted me, for you have ordered me to be hanged at eight o'clock tomorrow morning, so I am just going to cut your throat.'

I did not lose my presence of mind, and said quite calmly, 'Well, doctor, you are quite right; I was always your friend, and before you proceed to cut my throat, you may as well shake hands on it.'

'I will do that,' he said, and as I spoke, I was struggling as quietly as possible to get my arms from under the bedclothes.

'Give us your hand, old fellow,' I said, and he put his hand unhesitatingly into mine. I took a firm grip of it, and said quite quietly, 'Why, old fellow, you have given me the wrong hand; give us the other one,' which he immediately did. Keeping a tight hold of his hands, I gathered myself up in the bed, threw him flat on his back on the floor, with the whole of the bedclothes on the top of him, and ran for my life, leaving him in full possession of my tent. After that he had to be treated almost as a prisoner, with two soldiers to watch him night and day. At the first opportunity, he was sent down to Calcutta, where he remained in hospital for a long time, but ultimately recovered and was sent home to England.

About two days after the Residency was relieved, I received orders one morning to march in the direction of the Alum Bagh. (Of course, this was before Sir Henry Havelock's funeral, recorded earlier.) My regiment was the first to move off, and we were riding quietly along in front of everybody. I had not the least idea where we were going, except that we were told to go in that direction, when suddenly the commander-in-chief galloped up alongside of me, followed by his staff. He was evidently very much put out, and his first exclamation was to me, 'Throw out your leading troop in skirmishing order on the right flank.'

I immediately gave the order to the officer in command of the troop, and before the first word of command was almost out of his mouth, Sir Colin exclaimed, 'Who is that confounded useless infantry officer who does not know what to do?' I saw the colour mount in the officer's cheeks, but he never said a word like the good man that he was, and he happened to be a very smart cavalry officer who had been adjutant of his regiment, and was attached to us for drill purposes. Of course, he was doing exactly what he ought to have done, but Sir Colin was in a bad temper and ready to pitch into anybody.

He rode alongside of me for some time at the head of the regiments, and I felt very much like a mouse in the company of a large cat, for I did not know when I would be pounced upon, and I had no idea at the time that the whole army was behind us. We could hear distinctly a cannonade going on in the distance, and I learned afterwards that Sir Colin had just received a dispatch informing him of the ugly reverse which General Wyndham had received from the Gwalior contingent, as it was called, and that he had retired upon Cawnpore. I believe 'retired' is the correct expression for the occasion, as it was always used by the Russians when receiving a thrashing from the Japs.

After marching a few miles, Sir Colin turned round to me and said, 'Extend your regiment, sir, right across country, and allow nothing to pass through but the fighting men.'

To give you an idea of what he expected me to do with a couple of hundred men you have only to imagine a mob of many thousand camp-followers, carts, camels, elephants, and the whole of the commissariat equipment for the army, going on in a perfectly independent mob, everyone taking his own way and following the army. There was no particular road, and the country was quite open.

The last words that Sir Colin said were, 'See that you obey my orders, sir, for you once disobeyed me.'

I knew fine what he meant: it was at Calcutta, when we were discussing the equipment of my men, and I had strongly objected to their carrying their kits in a valise behind the saddle, and this he permitted me to abandon, as I had a great wish that the men should ride as lightly as possible; I never did believe in a cavalry horse being made a beast of burden. I proposed that the men's kits should be packed in their beds, as when a man cannot get his bed, he has very little necessity for a change of clothing. He requested me to let him have a list of what the men should carry with them on service. In the multiplicity of other things, I forgot to send him the list next morning, and had very soon a reminder. You see, Sir Colin looked upon the Military Train Cavalry almost as a child of his own, as he considered himself entirely responsible for our success or otherwise, and watched us most closely all through the campaign, an honour which I may say no other regiment but ours received.

As it had barely 200 men, it was a tremendously difficult task to keep the whole of the camp-followers of the army in check. As soon as the fighting men had passed, the mob commenced to arrive. My officers and non-commissioned officers were ordered to ride up and down, and the men were posted two and two at a considerable distance from each other. The order I gave was that no one on any pretext was to be allowed to pass through, and if any man attempted to do so he was to be cut down at once. Every moment the mob became greater, and the most troublesome men I had to deal with were the so-called sick men riding on elephants, who cursed at large and did their best to persuade the natives to break my line.

I took up a solitary position about 200 yards in front, facing the mob. Soon I saw an officer's servant—a native, of course—mounted on his master's horse, trying to force his way through. The regimental sergeant-major ordered him to go back, but in spite of that he broke through and came full gallop in my direction. I went for him at once, and he saw by my face that I was in dead earnest, and just escaped being run through by throwing himself off the horse while going at full gallop. Away went the horse with his tail in the air, and what became of him was none of my business. For one moment as I stood over the man sprawling on the ground, I felt terribly inclined to run him through, and he never had a closer escape for his life before. However, I ordered him to get up and return to the mob, and somewhat helped his movements with the point of my sword until he was ignominiously driven back into the line, and after that no one tried the experiment of breaking through.

When the order came that the camp-followers might advance, I simply made the left of the line which was nearest the army move quietly forward at a walk, and immediately the mob rushed behind us, and the whole stream made for the distant camp. I felt uncommonly relieved when they were all cleared off.

CHAPTER 12

Hodson's Horse at Work

Sir Colin Campbell went by forced marches to Cawnpore, leaving behind a division of about 4,000 men—cavalry, infantry and artillery—under the command of Sir James Outram, who encamped in front of the Alum Bagh and in the open country. There this little force remained for the whole winter, almost within reach of the guns of Lucknow, and holding in check an army of some 60,000 men, who occupied the city under the immediate command of the *ranee*—that is, the Queen of Oude, whose husband's acquaintance I had the pleasure of making in Fort William.

The Military Train formed part of this force—in fact, we were the only cavalry that Outram had, except the small body of volunteers, most of them gentlemen, whose occupation as civilians was, for the time being, gone.

It must be remembered that, though the Residency was relieved, the mutineers were still in possession of the town, which Sir Colin had good reason for not attempting to take at the time. He preferred leaving Outram to hold them in check, and splendidly that general did his work. He knew the native character well, having had long experience of their ways, and had a perfect knowledge of their language, and with the assistance of the all-powerful *rupee* he established an excellent system of information, and actually knew everything that went on in the town. When there was a council of war held by the enemy, he knew within a few hours all that had been resolved upon at it, and he was never once taken by surprise during the whole time we were stationed there. His system was delightfully simple. A message would reach us from him in the afternoon that he wished to see all the commanding officers at his tent, and then his address to us was generally this:

Hodson's Horse

Gentlemen, we are going to be attacked from such and such a quarter at daylight tomorrow morning; be ready in good time. Good-evening, gentlemen.

No long rigmarole or long words, but we knew exactly what he required from us. Not a drum was beaten or a bugle sounded on the following morning, but every regiment formed up on its own parade, the horses hooked into the guns, and all mounted men in their saddles. Then, just before daylight, Outram would come riding quietly up to every regiment in turn to see that all was correct. Our camp was on the extreme left flank, and nearly all the fighting took place in that direction. On the other flank was the Alum Bagh, well-fortified. It was simply a palace standing in a garden and surrounded by a strong wall. There was also a small fort known by the name of Jelalabad, which was occupied by a little force, and on this account our right flank was seldom, if ever, attacked, as the two forts would have made it rather warm for them.

As a rule, when a fight was in prospect, the general would ride quietly up to me, saying, 'Are you all right, Robertson?'

'All right, sir,' was my reply.

'Then send out a troop (or it might be a squadron) to look for the enemy.'

This was almost invariably the way in which the fighting began, and as the daylight came on, we could see a great line of skirmishers in the distance advancing towards the camp with the rest of the attacking force coming on behind. Then our artillery would gallop to the front, as a rule taking the enemy in the flank, and supported by our cavalry; and very often an artillery duel began and ended the fight, as their infantry very seldom came within range of ours.

We advanced steadily forward from our camp, and the enemy as steadily retired, getting the benefit of round shot or shell to hasten his retreat. When the general considered that he had gone far enough, he would turn quietly round and say, 'Gentlemen, we will now go back to breakfast.' This will give a general idea of the kind of skirmishing that went on from day to day, but sometimes, of course, it was a good deal hotter. On one occasion, when the enemy's artillery had got our exact range, I saw the general ride quietly up to one of our guns, and say to the man in charge of the port-fire, 'Oblige me with a light for my cigar'—taking no notice of the round shot that were whizzing past.

Our casualties, I am thankful to say, were few.

One evening, as I was riding in the vicinity of our advance post on the left front, I saw one of the enemy in the distance, armed with a shield and drawn sword, walking up to the sentry in front of the picket. The sentry immediately came to the charge with his bayonet. The man stopped just in front of him, and quietly put his sword in its scabbard. The sentry shouted for the sergeant of the guard, who immediately made a prisoner of the man, and sent him to the general in the charge of a corporal and two men. On arrival at the general's tent, he said, 'Let the man come in;' and in he walked, quite calmly, and made his report. This I found was the general's way of getting information, which was always absolutely correct.

If the information was of no great consequence, the general would call in his head man with a bag of *rupees*, and the native was allowed to put his hand in and take out as much as he could grasp, rolling the money up in his waistband. If the information was very important, he was allowed to dive in both hands. Then the general would order the corporal to march the man back to where he came from, and on arrival at the picket the man would walk quietly away into the darkness.

It was curious to see how these men were allowed to wear their swords, even when alone with the general. Some people would have felt rather uncomfortable, but General Outram was a man entirely devoid of fear. I have never seen his equal for calm coolness in all circumstances.

One morning, after receiving the usual instructions from Outram the previous afternoon, we moved off silently to the left of the camp, past the Alum Bagh, and out into the country, which was very much wooded by mango groves, and one could see but a short distance in any direction. After marching some way, the force halted, and the general sent my regiment forward to reconnoitre, saying, 'Go to a village which you will find on your right front, and see if it is occupied by the enemy.' So, on we went for some distance, when we came suddenly upon a party of the enemy's cavalry. They at once went off at a gallop in the direction of Lucknow, and we followed them; after a few hundred yards we came in sight of two of the enemy's guns, and they immediately wheeled and started in the same direction, and we at once followed the guns, leaving the cavalry to get clean away.

Of course, these did not attempt to protect the guns for a moment; we followed the guns at a furious gallop for a mile or two, gradually gaining on them, and a most exciting race it was. Suddenly the enemy came upon a deep ravine, and, either purposely or by accident, they capsized both the guns into it, and in an incredibly short time every horse was unhooked, and they went off at full gallop. They must have been splendidly trained gunners, from the way in which they got off. We followed, but only overtook and cut up a few of them who were not mounted, and then returned to the guns. We were now entirely alone, and out of sight of our own force, and a plucky enemy might have given us an ugly time of it. I sent back to inform the general that we had taken two guns, and wanted help to get them out of the *nullah*. After waiting what appeared a long time, I rode quietly up myself in the direction that I saw the Infantry coming. Fancy my surprise to see the skirmishers who were in front kneel down deliberately and take pot-shots at me as I sat all alone on my horse! Fortunately, they were uncommonly bad shots, and I was none the worse, but some of the bullets came very close.

I herewith append Sir James Outram's dispatch giving a full account of this day's fighting, and you will observe how honourably we were mentioned:

Camp, Alum Bagh,

December 2

Major-General Sir James Outram has much pleasure in recording in Division Orders his satisfaction with the conduct of the officers and men under the command of the Brigadier Stisted, engaged yesterday in the skirmish at Guilee, in which four guns and twelve waggons filled with ammunition were captured.

The right column, under the command of Lieutenant-Colonel Purnell, Her Majesty's 90th Regiment, consisting of detachments of the 78th and 90th Regiments, and of the Ferozepore Regiment of Sikhs, excited his admiration by the gallant way in which, with a cheer, they dashed at a strong position held by the enemy, and from which they were met by a heavy fire. Regardless of the overwhelming numbers, and six guns reported to be posted there, the suddenness of the attack, and the spirited way in which it was executed, resulted in the immediate flight of the enemy, with hardly a casualty on our side.

Colonel Guy, in command of the left column, consisting of 400 men of Her Majesty's 5th Fusiliers, under the guidance of Lieutenant Moorsom, Deputy-Assistant-Quartermaster-General, was equally successful in his simultaneous attack on the adjacent village of Guilee, in which and the adjoining tope two guns were captured.

The enemy were now rapidly followed up across the plain by the Volunteer Cavalry, under Captain Barrow, until they found refuge in a village, from which they opened a fire of grape and musketry. They were, however, speedily dislodged by the assistance of two of Captain Olpherts' guns, under the command of Lieutenant Smithett, and, changing their line of retreat, they endeavoured to reach the city by the way of the Dil Koosha.

The Military Train, under Major Robertson, having been, however, dispatched to make a flank movement, followed them up so rapidly that they dispersed their cavalry, and drove their guns into a ravine, where they were captured, the leading horses, of which the traces were cut, only escaping.

The major-general was particularly pleased with the very cool and soldier-like behaviour of the Military Train. Far ahead of the Infantry and unable to remove the guns which were captured, they were menaced in their front by a large body of fresh troops from the city, and attacked on their right flank by the main body of the enemy, consisting of about 2,000 infantry, who had commenced their march previous to our attack, and who, on having their rear assailed also, changed their route to one in the direction of the city, and seeing their guns in possession of so small a force as that under Major Robertson, made demonstrations of an attempt to regain them; but, by the bold front shown by the Military Train and the gallant advance of their skirmishers, were held at bay until the arrival of a party of the 5th Fusiliers, and two 9-pounder guns, under Captain Olpherts, completely secured their capture, and enabled a working-party of the Madras Sappers, under the command of Lieutenant Ogilvie, to extricate them from the ravine into which they had been driven. Captain Hutchinson, chief engineer, on this, as on several other occasions during the day, afforded much valuable assistance.

The major-general has to thank Lieutenant-Colonel H. Hamilton, commanding the reserve, for the good position taken up by him, which, with the fire of the two guns under Lieutenant Simpson, which were most judiciously posted, were of great assistance in checking the advance of the enemy during the protracted operations of removing the captured guns.

Sir James Outram has also to express his acknowledgments to

A Military Train Cavalry charge

Brigadiers Hamilton and Eyre, who were left in charge of the camp, and with the small force at their disposal checked the dispositions for an attack which the enemy were commencing with their skirmishers on the left flank, until the return of the force to camp caused them to abandon their intentions.

The major-general is happy to have to record his approval of the conduct of Staff-Sergeant Roddy, who was in command of the two guns attached to Colonel Guy's column, and whom his commanding officer, Captain Olpherts, has mentioned for the able way in which he brought his guns into action, and the good service he rendered in covering the rapid advance of the column.

Major Robertson has also brought to his notice the great assistance he received on every occasion from Captain Lane, 5th Bengal Light Cavalry, and Lieutenant Rich, Her Majesty's 9th Lancers, attached to the Military Train.

About this time the general thought we might greatly improve our food-supply by establishing a bazaar, and it was decided that it was to be set up in the rear of my camp. So, I got a flagstaff and mounted on the top of it my own special flag, which I used to have on board the *Lizzie*, only a good deal larger. It was a white flag with two long tails and a blue St. Andrew's Cross. As our uniform was blue and white this answered admirably, and a Kotwal was appointed to be in charge of the future bazaar, but unfortunately nobody came to sell, so I received orders from the general to see if I could establish a bazaar in my own way; therefore, before daylight on a very foggy morning I took the regiment about two miles from camp till we came to the main road leading into Lucknow. This was not the Cawnpore road, but one about two miles further to the left, as you face Lucknow. Then I formed one squadron across the road and extended a troop on each side, in the form of the letter 'V,' and so placed as to make a nice little trap to catch the natives as they came in with their supplies to sell at Lucknow.

After sitting some time, quite concealed by the fog, I heard voices, and a party of the villagers walked into the trap. Their surprise was very great and their alarm considerable, but I at once assured them that they were not going to be hurt, and that they had only to sit down where they were. This went on for half an hour, and the only amusing incident was that an old lady insisted on screaming at the top of her voice, till we rolled her head up in a cloth, when she subsided.

Having got as many natives as we required to form a market, and the fog beginning to rise, I recalled my men, and we went quietly back to the camp with the whole mob.

There I handed them over to the *kotwal*, (head man of military bazaar), and he arranged them in a long row under the flag, made them sit down and produce what they had to sell. Then he commenced at one end, saying, 'What value do you put upon that?'—pointing to what they had with them.

'One *rupee*,' the owner would reply.

'Then ask two for it, and do not sell it for less.'

In this way he went down the line and fixed the price of everything, directing them to ask a good deal more than the value. Then it was publicly announced that the bazaar was open. There was at once a rush of the officers' servants and others and native camp-followers, and in a very few minutes everything was sold, the *kotwal* taking care that everything was paid for in cash. Then he said, 'Now go home to your villages; you have all got your money. Come back tomorrow morning and you will be treated in the same way.'

And from that day we had a flourishing bazaar and quite cut out Lucknow, the villagers going and coming just as they pleased, for there was a strict order given in camp that no notice was to be taken even of the enemy's spies, and all were welcome to come and see everything there was to be seen.

Outram was a grand man, and thoroughly understood the native character.

The commissariat was running very short of beef, so the general ordered me to go into the country and catch cows where I could find them. Taking a band of commissariat men as drivers, we went off and scoured the country without being once interfered with by the enemy, although I had only a squadron with me and no artillery. In India cattle live in the villages to which they belong, and are quite tame, knowing their owners and their houses perfectly well, but are generally very wild towards strangers, and when out feeding during the day at a distance, the owners have only to give a well-known call, and the cattle come galloping home.

Knowing this we had to be particularly careful in the way we went to work.

Trotting along we would drive all the cattle we could find belonging to one village into a mob, and then proceed to another and collect in the same way. Sometimes they would break through and get home in spite of us—nothing would stop them.

Having passed the greater part of the day at this work, we got as many as we wanted and commenced to return to camp; but the cows did not see it in the same light, and we could not get them to go, neither by our native men nor by ourselves.

Just then an old lady came howling up from one of the villages, having recognised her cow in the mob, and as the animals were terribly unmanageable, a bright idea struck our interpreter (to whom I must apologise for not having brought him before the notice of the public sooner, and his invaluable services to the regiment during our stay in India), and he said to the old woman, 'You take your cow and walk in front of the mob, and then all the rest will follow; and then when we get to camp you shall have your cow back again.'

'All right,' said the old lady; 'done with you,' and she walked off smiling with her cow at the head of the mob, and we had no more trouble. What cared she if all the cows and bullocks in the country were eaten, as long as she got her own back again—her darling cow, which she simply hugged when she found that she could redeem it in this way.

It was certainly a comical day's work for cavalry to accomplish.

We kept some distance behind the drove, not to alarm them; but when quite near the camp what was our horror to see the whole mob coming back at full gallop, heads down and tails up! We shouted, yelled, and barked like dogs, but it was of no use. They came and dashed right through us, and how we escaped serious accidents I really do not know.

I rode back in a terrible state of disgust and went straight to the general's tent, and almost burst in on him as he was sitting at dinner with his staff, saying, 'Oh, general, we have lost all the cows!'

'My dear Robertson,' he replied, 'make your mind easy; we have got as many as we want quite safe, and those that you met were purposely turned loose.'

Beer at this time was at a high premium, and none was to be had for love or money, and the poor beer-drinkers were in a sad state. One happy possessor of a bottle poured out a foaming glass as we were sitting at mess.

'Look here,' said an officer across the table, 'I will give you a sovereign for that glass just as it stands.'

The lucky possessor took the glass up lovingly, looked at it, then shook his head and drank it off.

On February 25, 1858, and only a few days before Sir Colin Campbell arrived with the intention of capturing Lucknow, Outram, who had already been reinforced by several regiments of cavalry, was informed by his spies that the whole rebel army in Lucknow had resolved to come out before the arrival of Sir Colin, and wipe us clean out.

On this occasion we started at daylight and moved from the right of our camp, being the opposite direction from which attacks were generally made on us.

It was announced that the *begum* herself was coming out on an elephant with all the great men, and we had arranged with Captain Wyatt, an old Ceylon elephant hunter, who was a first-class shot, that he was to shoot the *begum's* elephant, and so make her prisoner.

We were leading the advance, Sir James riding with me, and when we got to a part which was thickly wooded, and where we could see no distance in any direction for the trees, the general said, 'Halt here till I send for you.' The rest of the army marched on, and we were left quite alone, forming in two squadrons at half-distance, and there we waited patiently for a long time. We could neither see nor hear anything, but we were under the impression that the battle had not yet begun.

Suddenly an officer came galloping up to me furiously, and said. 'There are two guns which have been annoying the Jelalabad Fort all the morning; you are to take them at once.'

'Where are the guns?' I asked. 'I will show you,' he said.

I replied, 'Come on.'

We started off at once, first at a trot and then at a gallop, when suddenly, to our great astonishment, we found ourselves on the right flank of the rebel army, some 30,000 strong, drawn up in a perfect line, as if on parade.

The officer who brought the order led us right along the front of the whole of this force, and only about 100 yards from them. Of course, the moment we appeared a tremendous fire was opened upon us, which lasted the whole length of the line. (General Outram's calculation afterwards was that there were eleven infantry regiments in this line.) A terrific running fire and a perfect hail of bullets streamed over our heads; but miraculously, I may say, throughout the whole of this gallop not a man or horse was hit, and the only casualty I could ascertain was a ball through the trumpet-major's trumpet.

When we arrived right at the other flank of the line, the officer who was conducting us, and riding alongside of me, said: 'There are the guns'—pointing to two guns, which were then in the act of being

170

loaded, and were being supported by a strong party of rebel infantry.

I gave the command, 'Left wheel, charge!' and we rode right at them.

A party of the rebels were drawing water at a well which stood in front of us, and every man of them jumped into the well.

I was leading in front of everybody, in the hope of getting at the guns before they were loaded. The first man I encountered was a fat old native officer who evidently commanded the supports. As I came towards him, he made a fierce cut at me with his *tulwar*, but missed his blow, and as I passed him at full gallop, I drew my sword across his naked throat and the blood spurted right up to the hilt of my sword. Instantly after this a second man cut at me, but I caught the blow on my sword, dropped my point, and ran him through the throat, breaking 6 inches off the end of my sword. At the same instant a man on the other side hit at me, fortunately missing his blow, and I struck him fair over the head, and dropped him.

Just then, about 10 yards in front of me, I saw a *sepoy* with his finger on the trigger of his musket, aiming directly at my chest. I swerved my horse sharp to the right, and called out in Hindustani to the man, 'Run away, and I won't hurt you.' For one instant he hesitated with his finger on the trigger, then threw the musket on his shoulder, and went off like a greyhound. He knew perfectly well that the moment he killed me he would have been killed himself by my own men, immediately behind. I always fought in an old blue quilted jacket over my uniform, and he evidently mistook me for a private soldier, and so I escaped his shot.

There was a short and sharp fight, and not a man of the enemy was left alive, except those who saved themselves by flight.

Fancy our astonishment when we saw almost the whole of this great army in full flight back to Lucknow; and as we stood by the guns we had captured, we had the pleasure of seeing a magnificent charge by Hodson's Horse, who went galloping in among the flying *sepoys*, doing splendid execution. They evidently had dashed forward on seeing our charge, and were in good time to do some excellent work.

I had time to look about me as we stood by the guns, and I found that my second antagonist had cut clean through the pommel of my saddle, and taken off the point of the toe of my boot, without inflicting the slightest wound either on myself or on my horse.

Just then Outram rode up to me, trying to look fierce, but I could see a bright twinkle in his eye that said quite the reverse. 'You are a pretty fellow,' he said, 'to go and fight a battle all by yourself, and spoil my plans.'

'Why, sir, I only obeyed your orders.'

'My orders! my orders, indeed!'

'Yes, general; you ordered me to take these two guns, and there they are.'

'Who dared to give you that order?' he said.

'There, sir,' I said—'there is the gentleman'—pointing with my sword to the officer who had conducted us.

Outram rode up to him at once, but what passed between them I never knew. I expect the officer got it hot.

Had the rebels been worth their salt they ought to have killed every one of us.

I had one poor fellow mortally wounded in the final charge on the guns, who came to me from the 17th Lancers, and rode in the celebrated charge at Balaclava. As he lay in hospital he said, 'It is very hard after being through the Balaclava charge to be shot by a n———r.'

Outram returned with his division to camp, but the cavalry were left some time on the ground to watch the enemy, in case they might think of returning.

One often hears people talk grandiloquently of the proudest day of their life, and I can safely say that that was the proudest day of mine; for as we returned back to our camp, we had to ride right along the front of the line; and as we approached, someone called out, 'Here are the Military Train; here they come;' and the men of the infantry regiments, whom we were passing at the time, came running out of their tents some with towels in their hands and some with handkerchiefs cheering wildly, and shouting, 'Bravo! bravo, Military Train!' patting the horses' necks and escorting us into our own camp. It was a spontaneous display of admiration at our gallant charge, which they had seen while formed up in order of battle.

Here is Sir James Outram's account of the day's fighting:

From Major-General Sir James Outram, C.B., commanding First Division, to the Deputy-Adjutant-General of the Army.

Camp, Alum Bagh,
6 February, 1858.

Sir,

I have the honour to report the particulars of the repulse of a determined demonstration which the enemy made on our

172

position yesterday, the 25th inst.

The principal attack was on our right, against which twenty four regiments of regular infantry, 6th Nujeeb Corps, 1,000 cavalry, and eight guns, moved out from the trenches; of this number about one-half, with two guns, advanced towards our right rear, and having occupied the topes immediately to the east of Jellalabad, commenced shelling that post heavily, evidently in the hope of igniting the large quantity of combustible stores at present collected there, while the remainder held in support the villages and *topes* directly in front of the enemy's outworks.

Large bodies of infantry and cavalry, with three guns, simultaneously menaced our left, and the trenches in front of our position were occupied in force.

Soon after 10 a.m. I moved out with detachments of artillery, cavalry, and infantry, as per accompanying return, to intercept the column which had opened its guns on Jellalabad, having previously sent Barrow's Volunteers and Wale's Horse round, *via* Nowrungabad, to co-operate in the rear.

As we advanced, a portion of the enemy's reserve made a demonstration against our left, but was speedily driven back, and afterwards held in check by the four guns of Remington's troop, supported by a squadron of the 7th Hussars, under Colonel Haggart, and by Brasyer's Sikhs.

The column then moved forward, flanked on the left by Brigadier Campbell with the native cavalry, which pushed on in advance to intercept the enemy's retreat, which, owing to their having heard the fire of Remington's guns, proved more sudden than we had anticipated. The manoeuvre was completely successful, and speedily converted their retreat into a rout. Brigadier Campbell's detachment assailed them on the one side, while Barrow's and Wale's Horse appeared on the opposite quarter, and the military train, under Major Robertson, dashed into the middle of the flying enemy and captured their two guns. The rapidity of their flight prevented the Infantry from taking a prominent part in the action. At 1 p.m., when we finally left the field, the foe had vanished.

In the meantime, the hostile forces on the left of my position had retired before the very effective fire of Moir's guns, not liking the looks of the arrangement, which had been prepared by

Brigadier Franklin, who had been left in command of the camp for their reception.

Judging from the corpses which strewed the field where the cavalry had charged, and from the dense masses upon which our guns repeatedly opened, the enemy's casualties must have been heavy. Our loss consisted of four men killed, five officers and twenty men wounded.

My cordial acknowledgments are due to all the officers and men who conducted and took part in these operations, but especially to the military train, whose brilliant charge excited the enthusiasm of all who witnessed it.

Colonel Berkeley, my noble and zealous military secretary, whose knowledge of the ground was of great service to Brigadier Campbell in cutting off the enemy's retreat, was wounded while gallantly charging at the head of Hodson's Horse, as was Lieutenant Moorsom while rendering to Barrow and Wale assistance similar to that which Colonel Berkeley afforded to the brigadier.

About 4 p.m. the enemy again moved out against us. On this occasion they directed their principal efforts against our left, and evinced more spirit and determination than they have hitherto done. Repeatedly they advanced within grape and musket range, and as they ever met with a warm reception from our guns and Enfields, especially from those of the left front picket, commanded by Major Master of the 5th Fusiliers, they must have suffered severely.

They renewed their fire from time to time during the night, but solely, I believe, with the object of covering the parties engaged in removing their dead. Our loss in this subsequent operation amounted to one man killed and fourteen wounded. In all, five men killed and thirty-five officers and men wounded.

The conduct of the troops throughout the entire day and night was excellent at every point, and merits the highest commendation.

The usual returns of ordnance captured, and of casualties, are hereby forwarded.

I have, etc.,

(Signed)   J. Outram, Major-General,
commanding First Division.

The only remark I would like to make about the general's dispatch is that *we* did not dash into the *flying* enemy, but actually *put* them to flight; and the moment that Hodson's Horse saw our charge *they* dashed into the flying rebels, making one of the grandest charges that could be conceived, and as I sat on my horse beside the two captured guns, I could see them cutting and slashing in all directions. They were a splendid body of men, and behaved magnificently.

I may add that the general ordered the two guns which we had taken to be planted in front of our camp as an honour.

yours faithfully

J.J. Robertson

CHAPTER 13

In Hospital at Calcutta

Shortly after the cattle-lifting expedition I was sent off with an immense convoy of empty waggons down to Cawnpore to bring up stores and provisions, including ammunition.

It was a very important charge, and I was very proud of getting it, as I was the youngest commanding officer in the whole force.

I had with me cavalry, infantry, and artillery, and the train of waggons covered miles of the road. Everything passed off satisfactorily, but in returning, when we were one march off the camp, I received an urgent pencil note from Colonel Napier, afterwards Lord Napier of Magdala, then chief of the staff, as follows:

> Come on straight tonight, as the enemy has arranged to attack you in great force tomorrow morning.

So instead of resting as usual at Bunee Bridge, which was a day's march from the Alum Bagh, we made a forced march all that night, and I am happy to say that I got everything landed in camp before daylight, and the enemy was just an hour or two late.

It was after Sir Colin Campbell arrived for the purpose of taking Lucknow that the following very disagreeable affair took place: I was handed over to the brigadier, who commanded the whole of the cavalry, and who had the reputation of being one of the smartest cavalry officers in the service.

When at dinner with Sir James Outram, this officer, whose name I prefer not to mention, commenced to abuse my men in very strong language. Colonel Napier stopped him short, remarking very pointedly, 'I know and I have seen what Robertson and his men can do, and I won't sit here and have them run down. If you ever do as well, you may thank your stars.'

177

Of course, from that moment he was my deadly enemy, although I had never even spoken to him, and he took the earliest opportunity of showing his ill-will.

A day or two after, an order came from Sir Colin Campbell, who was then operating against Lucknow, to say that the whole of the enemy's cavalry, 5,000 strong, had broken out of the city, and that our cavalry were to go in pursuit. Fancy my surprise at receiving the order to remain in and take charge of the empty camp with a handful of men while the Military Train of which I was the commanding officer was taken as part of the force, under the command of Captain Wyatt, the next senior officer. Had such an order of the brigadier's appeared in the public papers, everyone would have said, 'That senior officer is not fit for his post, and so has had to be left behind,' so on and so on. About an hour after the cavalry had gone off, I received an urgent message from the officer commanding in the absence of Sir James Outram (who had gone with Sir Colin on account of his knowledge of the city); the dispatch ran as follows:

The whole of the enemy's cavalry are coming to attack the camp; do the best you can.

I mustered about twenty of my own men, all that were left me, and about the same number of the 7th Hussars, and the paymaster of the 7th—a fine old soldier—took command of his men. The doctor hurriedly armed all his sick men on the top of a small mud tower that we had erected ourselves for a look out.

There were also two guns in camp in charge of Lieutenant Smithett. Before describing what follows, I must give the reader an idea of the surroundings.

The camp faced Lucknow, and was protected in the rear by a swamp. Our camp was on the left face. Thrown back at right angles to the main line, and immediately in front of it, about 400 yards off, was a small village which had been converted into a picket. Taking the picket as a centre, a deep ditch had been cut right away in the direction of Lucknow, and on the other side of the picket in the same line was an abattis of felled trees, but between the end of the trees and the picket about 50 yards were left perfectly open for the passage of troops, and that was the way we always went out to fight on that side through the gap. Both the ditch and abattis were quite impassable for either cavalry or artillery, and therefore the open passage was the key of our position.

I had scarcely got my men mounted, when we could see dust in the distance. We trotted into the gap with the two guns on our right, and formed a living gate—the only chance of protecting the camp.

We had just got into position when the whole body of the enemy's cavalry approached us at a wild gallop, waving their swords fiercely in the air. The ground actually shook as they came on at us. We sat perfectly still; the paymaster and myself sat in front of our men as if waiting to receive a general officer.

On they came till the head of the column was within 50 or 60 yards of us, then Smithett banged off his two guns, and I gave the word, 'Draw swords,' and out they flashed in the sun. The leading troop, not liking our appearance, wheeled to the right, and the whole body of the enemy's cavalry galloped furiously after them. The dust cleared away, and thus we saved the camp.

Some hours after, the gallant general of cavalry above referred to returned to camp with his whole force, never having seen any of the enemy. Of course, he did not think it necessary to report the stand that the little handful of men had made; we did not even get thanked for what we had done,

Here is my dispatch:

Camp, Alum Bagh,
March 17, 1858.

Sir,

I have the honour to report, for the information of the brigadier commanding, that on seeing the enemy's cavalry come out of the topes at a gallop in great force yesterday, I took out at a gallop Lieutenant Smithett's two guns, supported by a troop of the military train and a small detachment of the 7th Hussars under command of Lieutenant Gurforth, to the left picket, upon which the enemy were moving, apparently with a view of sweeping through our deserted camp. I formed the cavalry in the gap between the abattis and trench and the two guns on my right, which by their spirited fire brought the enemy to a halt, and after a few rounds he began to move towards our rear, at first slowly, but on Major Olpherts coming up with four more guns—two of which he placed to the right of the picket, and the other two on my left—the enemy improved his pace, apparently with the intention of coming round more quickly on the rear.

Most fortunately, at that moment, a squadron of the military train appeared, coming into camp in that direction, and the bold front which Captain Wyatt showed kept this vast horde at bay. I quickly reinforced him with two guns under Lieutenant Timbrell and the small detachment of Hodson's Horse, which fortunately came up at this moment, and advanced my centre and right divisions of guns with a party of Infantry in skirmishing order between them. Major Olpherts opened a splendidly directed fire upon the enemy, which soon sent him out of range, while a body of the enemy's infantry advanced and carried off their killed and wounded. About this time, Colonel McIntyre, of the 78th Highlanders, assumed the command.

The greatest credit is due to the handful of officers and men for their gallantry and steadiness at a time when destruction appeared almost inevitable. I never saw so large a body of cavalry assembled before, and have no idea of what their numbers were. They had only to advance to have swept us off the face of the earth.

       (Signed)   J. P. Robertson, Major.

A day or two after, the cavalry received orders to march again. This time I went with my regiment. No one knew where we were going or what we had to do; we simply rode along all day almost without halting. My friend the brigadier, of course, put us in the rear.

Captain Wale, who commanded a regiment of Irregular Cavalry (Wale's Horse), and I were riding together, when we saw a party of the enemy on the edge of a wood some distance to our right. Soon we saw one of Wale's men, a native, galloping in that direction from the brigadier-general. When he got pretty close to these men, who were mounted, he wheeled short round and came back at a gallop to his own commanding officer. He pulled up, presented to Captain Wale a little note, and said, 'The brigadier sent me with this note to those people over there, but they are the enemy, and as the general does not know a word of my language, I have come to you, sir, to report.'

Wale immediately galloped forward to the brigadier-general and told him how things were.

We read the note, which was as follows:

This is ——'s force; who are you?

'Oh, indeed,' said our leader, and rode on as if nothing had happened. We kept riding on all day in what appeared to be an aimless kind of fashion.

When the brigadier-general called a halt, we stopped, and just in front of where the 7th Hussars were there was an old house. I was close to it, when there suddenly rushed out of the house five or six fanatics with drawn swords, who made straight at a poor young officer who was sitting on his horse in front of his troop. He drew his pistol and shot the first man almost in a moment. I am sorry to say that before anyone could rush forward to help him, he was chopped to pieces before our eyes. Of course, the attackers had a short shrift.

Some little time after this we found ourselves on a rising ground, overlooking the River Goomti; this river passes round Lucknow, which was on our right, not far off.

The column halted, I know not why, except that the river was in front of us, and soon it appeared that neither brigadier nor staff was with us. This was a funny state of affairs, so the commanding officers met and discussed the matter, and arranged that we should form up in order of battle, to await events.

There we remained for some time, and as we were entirely without orders, we simply sat still; no one knew why we were there—or where we were, for that matter, except that we could see Lucknow in the distance. We could also see a great many people hurrying past between us and the river, which was deep and unfordable. They looked uncommonly like fighting men and inhabitants of the town all mixed up pell-mell together, but as they did not fire at us, we simply waited and looked at them.

After nearly all the people had passed, the brigadier-general suddenly appeared, looking quite smart and fresh, having had a good lunch, and having left us all that time to take care of ourselves.

He immediately ordered the 7th Hussars to charge the enemy. No one else was sent, and it was clear that they were to have it all to themselves.

I may mention that the ground in front of us was somewhat wooded, and it was difficult to see what was going on, or who the people were that the hussars were ordered to attack.

Away went the hussars at a gallop, and soon we heard a most extraordinary noise.

'What *can* that be?' we said. We distinctly heard screams, and then unmistakable laughter—'*Ha! ha! ha!*'

'What can it be?' we repeated. The cavalry had charged a mob of old washerwomen carrying their clothes on their heads! No wonder the men laughed, and I am happy to say they halted in time, so that not a single woman was hurt. This fully accounted for the laughter we heard.

This was the way our gallant brigadier-general carried out his orders, which—we afterwards heard—were that he was to intercept the garrison of Lucknow as they were driven out of the town; the result, however, was that the whole garrison escaped and we, the unfortunate Britishers, had to go through the miseries of a hot-weather campaign. Sir Colin Campbell was furious when it was reported to him, and my friend (?) was promptly sent to Cawnpore in disgrace, and was not allowed to take any further part in the campaign. I think my insult was satisfactorily avenged, and we saw no more of that officer. This incident is described by Captain Trotter in his *Life of Outram* as 'The Brigadier's Keen Pursuit.' So much for history.

The day after Lucknow was in our possession, I rode over from our camp to see Sir Colin Campbell. He was sitting at the door of his tent, and gave me quite a warm welcome. Almost the first thing he said to me was, 'I wrote home to the commander-in-chief about you the other day.' I made a polite bow, not knowing what was coming, and he went on: 'I told him you were just the kind of chap I wanted here, that you made no bones about anything.' Then he continued: 'Here's Russell coming over to breakfast; come in and have some.' This was the well-known and famous Russell of *The Times*, whose letters from the Crimea did untold service for the British Army by exposing the shortcomings and misdirected efforts of the authorities at home. He is now (1906), Sir William Russell, D.S.O., etc.

I knew Russell well in the Crimea, and he and his wife and family have been life-long friends of ours. May he be long spared to enjoy the well-earned title conferred upon him by Her Gracious Majesty in recognition of his long and faithful service to a grateful country! In the Crimea he and I had sat together once for the greater part of a night, on Cathcart's Hill, admiring the sight of the Russian fleet being burned by their own hands. I have now a pair of candlesticks made by a brother officer out of a portion of one of these ships.

Shortly after this Sir Colin started off with the greater part of his army in pursuit of the rebels who ought to have been cut off by us during their escape out of Lucknow. A force was organised for Sir Edward Lugard to go south with a view of dispersing the rebels in that direction, and I had the honour of commanding his Cavalry and having pretty hard work, as we were out fighting and marching the whole of the hot weather. We were constantly out scouting in all directions generally with half a troop of Royal Horse Artillery, and usually a squadron or so of my own men but had very little real fighting.

On one occasion, I remember, we saw a large party of the enemy making for a walled village. I directed a shell to be dropped among them before they got safely in. I said to the sergeant who was laying the guns, 'Make haste, sergeant, or it will be too late.'

To which he quietly answered, 'Ah, sir, this isn't Woolwich Common!' However, the shell was beautifully dropped among them.

On our way back we found the jungle occupied in force between ourselves and the camp, so I sent my trumpet-major to ask for a regiment of infantry. There was an impassable *nullah* on one side, and thick jungle within 50 yards all along towards camp, which made it impossible to ride down about a mile, with the enemy in full possession of the jungle. They tried to outflank us, and I had to dismount a troop to keep them in check. It was a very nasty position to be in, but after what seemed an age, the 10th Regiment made its appearance in skirmishing order, and the enemy took to their heels. As they ran, we charged them, and it was in this charge that Lieutenant Crawford was killed—an able and valuable officer promoted from the ranks. This kind of work went on all through the hot weather, in accordance with the direct orders of the commander-in-chief.

As the rebels were commanded by the well-known Koor Singh, we had to keep pegging away until our whole force was completely exhausted.

As we approached Azimghur, I received rather an extraordinary order, which was, to ride forward and see if the enemy were in possession of the town. When we arrived at the first gate, we found it open, and we had to ride through the narrow streets with tall houses on both sides. Had the enemy been there, this would have been an uncommonly awkward position for cavalry to be in. However, orders had to be obeyed, so I drew my revolver (I think the only time I had it out during the whole campaign), and rode at the head of the regiment, keeping a bright look out at the upper windows on both sides, expecting every moment to see muskets thrust out. I had made up my mind what to do, and had warned the men accordingly that if I fired my pistol—which I should have done at the first man who put his musket out of the window—the regiment were instantly to go threes about and gallop out of the town, as it would have been madness to push on any further.

However, as good luck would have it, the enemy had already evacuated the town on our approach, so we rode quietly from one gate to the other, and in due time the infantry followed us. Here we halted for some time, and a small party under command of Captain Wyatt went in pursuit of Koor Singh. When they came up with the enemy, they immediately charged, and a *sepoy* rebel shot one of my men's horses dead, the man being thrown violently forward, falling at the feet of his adversary. The *sepoy* dropped his musket, drew his sword, and cut him down with all his force over the head; but fortunately, we wore good thick turbans, and the sword did not penetrate his head.

In an instant my soldier jumped up and hit the *sepoy* fair in the wind, which, of course, would have been a foul blow in fair fighting, but quite allowable in such a case as this. Before the *sepoy* recovered his breath, my man grappled with him, wrenched the sword out of his hand and killed him with it. When Major Wyatt's party returned, this plucky fellow presented me with the sword, which I now have. It was a cavalry officer's sword which had, no doubt, belonged to some poor man who had been murdered during the early stages of the Mutiny. For this he was awarded the Victoria Cross. I regret very much that I cannot give his name, having forgotten it.

About this time Lugard reported to the commander-in-chief that he had carried out his orders, but a peremptory order came back to say he was to go on fighting, which we did until the rainy season set in.

One morning I was ordered to go with my usual little force, and make out the route to a certain place.

It was quite a long march, and in the afternoon, I returned and reported my success, to which Lugard was pleased to say, 'I was sure you could do it.'

Next morning, I conducted the forces along the way I had been the day before. We arrived at a slight eminence about the middle of the day, and in front of us was a perfectly level plain, upon which rice had been grown; but at that season it was completely hardened and dried.

Rice, as is well known, is always sown under water; in its early stages every field is surrounded by a little embankment, which holds in the water until the rice has somewhat got ahead.

Beyond the rice-fields was a continuous belt of jungle, extending in a straight line as far as we could see; but there was no sign of any enemy about, so the quartermasters were ordered to the front to mark out the ground, and we duly encamped, about 200 yards from the jungle. In a very short time almost everyone was asleep, when suddenly a rattling volley of musketry came from the enemy out of the jungle, the bullets spattering into the camp in all directions. Up everybody jumped. I shouted, 'Turn out sharp!' and in a very short time we were all mounted, scarcely a single man being properly dressed. I was simply in a pair of pyjamas and a flannel shirt, with a sword in my hand.

The infantry presented much the same appearance, and almost without any word of command the men rushed down to the jungle and commenced to fire away, and in a very few minutes the enemy scampered off, and left us to continue our sleep.

Not having been field-officer for the day, I have no idea how the sentries and pickets were posted, as that was not part of my duty. We afterwards ascertained that the enemy had been sitting in the jungle while were pitching our camp, and were quite puzzled as to what our intentions were.

The next day, as General Lugard had received information that the enemy were coming back, we formed in order of battle. I was in command of the left wing, and some little distance away from the main body. Everything was perfectly silent, and there was no appearance of an enemy, when Havelock, who was on Lugard's staff (we used to call him 'young Havelock,' in distinction from his gallant father, whose death, you may remember, I recorded after the relief of Lucknow) came galloping up to me at a tremendous pace—as his custom always was, being one of the most impetuous officers I ever met with—the order, 'You are to advance, sir, and begin the battle'—or words to that effect.

To which I replied, 'Please tell the general there is nobody to fight with.'

Back he came again to me at a gallop. The order was, 'You are to advance, sir.'

My little force consisted of a regiment of Madras Riflemen, my own men, and two guns. I immediately threw the riflemen into skirmishing order, and ordered them to advance.

The cavalry quietly followed them up, although it is difficult to imagine what possible use we could be, as we could not even have ridden into the jungle, much less charged. After the riflemen had advanced a short distance, a spattering fire commenced. The enemy were there after all, and as we halted outside, the bullets came flying through the trees, and we were in quite a shower of leaves as they came down, but not a shot touched us; they were all at the usual angle of 45 degrees. Soon the enemy retired, and we were ordered quietly back to camp.

An amusing incident occurred at headquarters. My orderly, Sergeant McQuestion by name, was on that occasion acting as orderly to the general. The little man was far too valuable to be allowed to go into action, and he was always left behind in camp, as he had, like all other orderly-room sergeants, an unlimited amount of writing to do. On this occasion he found himself mounted on a strange horse, sitting behind the general—not at all comfortable, I should suppose. Presently the general gave him an order to take to one of the regiments.

Away he started, all by himself, and in passing round some bushes, he came face to face with Havelock, who was galloping back to the general. McQuestion unfortunately mistook him for one of the enemy, pulled out his pistol, and fired right at his face. The explosion of his own pistol tumbled McQuestion flat on his back, and he had to pick himself up and walk back without a horse. Happily, he missed Havelock clean.

After the fighting Havelock came to me in a wild state of excitement and related the adventure, and I need not say that that was McQuestion's first and last battle.

The most remarkable feature of this memorable fight was that, to the best of my belief, there was not a single man either killed or wounded on our side.

The heat of a Bengal summer is something dreadful to be exposed to in the open, and the thermometer occasionally stood in the coolest of our tents at 125 degrees in the shade. I myself was so exhausted and reduced that I had to get a chair to mount my horse, and had to steady myself by the holsters. I could not even handle my sword with any comfort, though I was only thirty-six then!

I used to carry a large white umbrella instead of a sword, and I well remember my last day on horseback. We were as usual away from all supports by ourselves, and discovered a large body of the enemy waiting for us—a very unusual proceeding on their part, but I soon discovered the reason.

They were on the far side of a deep *nullah*, quite impassable for either cavalry or artillery.

I made my arrangements accordingly. Placing the two guns just behind the centre of the squadron (one squadron and two guns being our whole force), I gave all the necessary orders, and carefully instructed everyone as to what I intended to do, and we then charged at a gallop. When close to the *nullah*, the two troops wheeled outwards—by word of command—to the right and left, and almost before the wheel was completed, the artillery unlimbered and gave the enemy grape-shot and shell. The pace at which they scampered off was a sight to see.

On returning back towards camp, I fell off my horse on to the hot sand on the banks of the Ganges, and knew nothing more until I found myself on board a steamboat, in which I was taken to Benares, and safely lodged in the hospital there. I can just remember when the steamer stopped that I was taken out, and placed sitting at the feet of a lady in a buggy.

She supported me against the seat with both hands till we arrived at the hospital. It was a most kindly act, and I very much regret that I never knew who she was.

It was a comfort to be once more under a roof with the benefit of a *punkah* going night and day.

When slightly convalescent I was sent down by water to Calcutta in a passing steamer, and there I had a very dangerous relapse, and was carried to Mountains Hotel. My faithful bearer stuck to me through thick and thin, but all the other servants left, my *kitmutgar* being three months in arrears of wages. I asked the hotel people to send for a doctor, but this they shamefully refused to do, unless I wrote a note. In the condition which I then was this was quite out of the question. However, after they had positively refused in what I considered a most brutal manner, my servant brought me a scrap of paper and a pencil, and I managed to write:

Very ill; come and see me.

He went off to the officers' hospital, and immediately a doctor came and removed me there, where I remained for some weeks, hovering between life and death. However, my strong constitution got the best of it, and I began to recover.

While I was still in hospital both Sir Edward Lugard and Sir James Outram came to see me and expressed their sympathy. Sir James Outram I never saw again, but Sir Edward became permanent Secretary to the War Office, where I had many a chat with my old captain in after-years.

When I became convalescent, I was permitted sometimes by the doctor to be taken out for a short airing in the evening. A kind lady used to come in her carriage every evening to the hospital and send up word to the doctor that she was prepared to take any invalid officer for a drive.

One afternoon, Sir James Outram himself came with his carriage and drove me down to his house at Garden Beach, and introduced me to Lady Outram.

My fellow-companion in the room in the hospital was a Doctor Boyd who had been in the Residency at Lucknow along with Havelock and Outram. He used to give me most interesting details of his experiences and the horrors of that time, and we went home afterwards together in the same ship to England.

Having gone before a Medical Board at Calcutta I was ordered home. I went and took a passage on board a P. and O., for which I paid the sum of £90, as they had a complete monopoly at that time of the overland route.

On board I met a nice little party of four—Mr. and Mrs. Stewart; Mrs. Pillains, who was going home ill, having left her husband behind her at Calcutta, and was placed under the Stewarts' care; and the fourth was the Hon. Frederick Bruce, afterwards K.C.B., who was returning from China, where he had been our representative. They kindly asked me to join the party, and took the greatest care of me all the way home.

After an uneventful passage on board the P. and O. we duly arrived at Southampton, and going up to town I again appeared before a Medical Board, and had my leave extended till the arrival of the regiment from India. I may mention that when they embarked from Calcutta a salute was fired in their honour as a mark of the appreciation of our services during the Mutiny.

I append herewith a copy of the *Calcutta Gazette Extraordinary* which appeared on Saturday, April 23, 1859, No. 573 of 1859:

Notification.

Fort William, Military Department,
April 22, 1859.

The 2nd Battalion Military Train is under orders for immediate embarkation for England.

The career in India of this corps has been short but brilliant, and eminently serviceable to its country.

Upon arriving at the Presidency, it was at once converted into a Cavalry force, and sent untrained into the field under the late Sir Henry Havelock.

Throughout the glorious and most trying summer campaign, of which the first relief of Lucknow was the fruit, the Military Train bore a part which would have reflected credit upon the oldest and most experienced cavalry soldiers.

It has since served with distinction in various affairs under Lieutenant-General Sir James Outram—at the capture of Lucknow, in the operations about Azimghur, and lastly in the harassing campaign of Shahabad.

The Military Train leaves India with the best wishes of the Viceroy and Governor-General in Council for the future honour and prosperity of the battalion.

A salute will be fired from the guns at Fort William on the departure of the corps.

By order of His Excellency the Viceroy and Governor-General of India in Council.

R. J. H. Birch, Major-General,
Secretary to the Government of India

Here also I give a copy of Sir James Outram's farewell letter to me when the regiment was handed over to serve with General Lugard:

Lucknow,
March 28, 1858.

My Dear Robertson,

Permit me on the eve of your departure, in bidding you farewell, to send you an expression of the gratitude I owe you for the valuable services you have rendered me, and of my personal regard.

In my dispatches I have endeavoured, though I fear imperfectly, to give utterance to the admiration which the glorious conduct of your corps, under your own gallant and brilliant leading, has inspired me, and all that now remains for me to do is to assure you that you and they will ever be remembered by me with feelings of high esteem and warm regards.

To your officers individually pray tender my most hearty wishes for their welfare, and believe me ever,

Your and their sincere friend,
(Signed)   J. Outram.

As for myself, I was promoted to lieutenant-colonel after only eleven months as a major, and for the capture of Lucknow and the campaign was made a Companion of the Bath. Her Gracious Majesty, Queen Victoria, sent for me twice to Windsor to decorate me with her own fair hands, but each time I was unfortunately too ill to go.

Herewith I record a copy of the original summons to Windsor:

Heralds' College,
Doctors' Commons,
November 19, 1858.

Sir,

I am commanded by His Royal Highness the Prince Consort, Great Master of the Order of the Bath, to request your attendance at Windsor Castle on Monday next, the 22nd instant, at a quarter past two o'clock, Her Majesty having been pleased to signify her gracious intention to deliver to you, on that day, the insignia of a Companion of that Most Honourable Order. I have the honour to be, sir,

Your most obedient, humble servant,

Albert Woods,
Gentleman Usher of the Order.

An answer is requested.

Lieutenant-Colonel Robertson, C.B.

However, sometime after, when serving at Aldershot, I had the honour of dining with Her Majesty; Prince Albert and the Duke of Edinburgh were at the table, and Lady Churchill was the lady-in-waiting. All four are now gone, and I am still to the fore. It may be remembered that Lady Churchill died within a few days of Her Majesty.

After dinner, and when we retired to the drawing-room, Her Majesty came round to each guest and held a short conversation with them. I remember she gracefully expressed her satisfaction at the way in which my regiment had behaved throughout the Indian Mutiny. Prince Albert also came and said a few words, and I must be pardoned if I have much pleasure in recording this little event. Having recovered my health partially, I had previously attended one of Her Majesty's levees, and kissed hands.

In five years, by the rules of the service, after serving as lieutenant colonel in command of regiment, I was gazetted full colonel in the army.

After seven years' service in that rank, a Liberal and highly economical Government resolved to disband the Military Train, and in its place, they organised a new corps under the designation of the Army Service Corps, which was to be non-combatant and non-purchase.

Having by this time become commandant of the corps, with six battalions under me, I had the disagreeable duty of disbanding it. This was in 1870, and immediately after that duty was performed, having a great objection to being placed on half-pay with the prospect of seven years' or more idleness before my becoming a general, I exchanged with the colonel of the 16th Lancers for the purpose of selling my commission, the colonel of the 16th Lancers being anxious to be placed on half-pay.

As I appeared in the same *Gazette* as having exchanged into the 16th Lancers, and a little lower down the page as having sold out of the army, it is rather a puzzling question how long I was in that regiment.

The treatment which the Military Train received on being disbanded by a Liberal Government, in which Viscount Cardwell was Secretary of State for War, was perhaps the meanest and shabbiest act ever performed by any government.

Some twelve years before, when the corps was first raised, a donation of £200 was given to each battalion to provide themselves with cooking utensils, knives and forks, etc., for the mess. Well, when we were disbanded twelve years afterwards, we were ordered to refund that money to a grateful country, and literally had to sell all our mess property to satisfy this rapacious demand. Of course, everything had been worn out and replaced at our own expense at least three times during that period.

Some of the non-commissioned officers were treated in even a worse manner on the score of economy. Sergeant Shields had enlisted into the cavalry for twenty-three years' service, and according to the bargain which the nation had made with this man, he was entitled afterwards to a pension of half a crown a day for life. He had been a sergeant for many years, had an unblemished record, never having committed the slightest offence during the whole of his military service, not even the smallest military offence being recorded against him during all these years (almost a unique record), yet because he had not quite finished his twenty-third year, although perfectly able to serve, and having attained the rank of troop-sergeant-major, he was discharged and that without his own consent, and deprived of sixpence a day for life, because he had not served out his twenty-three years in full! I simply call it disgraceful. I could give several other instances almost as bad, but refrain.

For his valuable services to his country, Mr. Cardwell was made a viscount!

Having sent in my papers to sell my commission, as the phrase went in those days, I proceeded to wind up the Military Train, having, as I stated before, served in it from the very beginning, and raised two battalions. Now, as commandant, I sat down in solitary dignity in the office, and being, I may say, the last man of the corps, I proceeded to wind up the affairs. All the valuable documents were packed up and dispatched to the War Office, and those that were considered useless were sent down to the Royal Arsenal, Woolwich, to be converted into pulp, for paper in those days was much more valuable than it is now, and was not to be seen sticking in every hedgerow in the vicinity of towns, as at present.

I then proceeded to hand over my office to the Barrack Department, left my cards P. P.C. on the general and his staff, and quietly took my departure.

As I still suffered from the effect of sunstroke, I had received in India fully thirteen years previously, my wife and I proceeded to Shetland, where we spent a very enjoyable summer, as in those days, tourists were almost unknown there.

Some of my readers may remember the exciting story of a voyage which an old lady, Mrs. Elizabeth Mowatt by name, made all alone in a cutter from Shetland to Norway. Previous to her adventure it was in this very cutter that my wife and I sailed to Boddam, where we took up our residence, there being a delightful lake close by, well stocked with large trout. The sea-fishing was also very enjoyable in the long summer evenings, the sun only disappearing for a short time, and we were never deprived of daylight.

But to return to Mrs. Elizabeth Mowatt and her eventful journey. She was going from Lerwick to Boddam, and took her passage on this same cutter that we had sailed in. We knew the captain well, as his wife was our landlady's daughter. They started from Lerwick with a nice fresh breeze. Mrs. Mowatt was put down into the hold, or lower deck, I may call it, as it was decked over for the convenience of carrying small packages. Having got her down, they pulled up the ladder.

About half-way on the passage the captain was knocked overboard by the boom. The other two sailors (the crew consisted of three men altogether) launched the little boat, jumped in, and pulled their best in the direction where the captain had fallen overboard, forgetting in their haste to lash the helm. When they arrived near about the place, the poor captain had gone to the bottom, and after waiting for some little time, looking about anxiously, they reluctantly gave up the search as hopeless and prepared to return to the cutter. What was their horror to see her sailing before a fine, fresh, northeast breeze. They rowed frantically after her, but the cutter went much faster than they could row, and ultimately went clean out of sight. They then, of course, had to return to land and report what had happened.

To return to Mrs. Mowatt. It afterwards appeared that she knew nothing of what had happened, and thought bitterly that she had been deserted and left alone on board the cutter.

For days—I am not prepared to say how many—the poor thing remained a prisoner in the hold, with nothing to eat and nothing to drink, and actually was reduced to licking the moisture off a pane of glass.

Ultimately the cutter ran on shore on a small island off the coast of Norway. The circumstances were almost miraculous, for the Norwegians said afterwards that they would have been afraid to navigate a boat between the rocks. As the cutter grounded at high water, she was left almost dry when the tide went down. Two boys discovered her, and seeing nobody on board, waded out to her; and what was their astonishment to find an old lady in the hold, who could not speak a word of their language. However, they ran off and got assistance, and she was safely landed in Norway.

The island is only a few miles to the north of Aalsund, and I have frequently passed it on my way to Trondhjem.

An interpreter was fetched from Aalsund, and then the poor old lady told her story, and was ultimately restored to her home.

As soon as this adventure became known, Elizabeth was offered a sum of money by some enterprising company to exhibit herself in public; this she most indignantly refused to do.

One of the most interesting episodes in my life, which I greatly value, and now record, was being present at the Veterans' Parade held at Edinburgh Castle in 1903, when the king himself met us in the informal manner which showed his confidence in his old soldiers.

I should like to relate my personal experiences of the day, which was hailed with so great a pride and excitement by the veteran soldiers of the British Empire.

I went up to Edinburgh on the morning of May 3, and found that romantic city in a state of the wildest excitement as I walked towards the castle, with the eleven decorations recording my military career pinned on to my frock-coat for the occasion.

At the entrance to the Castle Parade I had to show my permit, with name, etc., recorded on it, and then, and not till then, could I pass in to the Crown Square, where the king was to receive us. There I found Sergeant-Major Masterson, late of the Scots Greys, on whose capable shoulders all the burden of the detail of the arrangements had fallen; in fact, it was mainly owing to his exertions that the proposal to hold such a review had been placed before Sir Archibald Hunter, and especially before the Marquis of Tullibardine, without whose ardent support the matter could not have been carried through.

Masterson deserves high praise for the indefatigable manner in which he, with Miss Masterson as secretary, worked night and day to collect from all parts of the country the body of veterans who composed the parade.

On arrival at the Crown Court, I found Masterson hard at work arranging the men, with a long list in his hand.

I was placed at the right of the line in consequence of my representing the oldest veteran on the parade, being the only officer (or man) who had been through the first great Sikh War under Sir Hugh Gough.

I, however, yielded my place to General Burroughs, late of the 93rd, and to two other generals.

The arrangement thus made was sadly marred by Colonel Duff finding it necessary to change the order of the parade from its position at the Banqueting Hall to the far end of the Crown Court; this resulted in what looked almost like a rout for the veterans, who were hustled up into an irregular mob some four or five deep; the roll-call was, as a matter of course, quite upset.

The rest of the square remained quite empty, there being no generals or staff present, and so we stood patiently waiting, when into the square a carriage and pair drove quietly, the scarlet liveries of the coachman and single footman alone denoting the presence of our king and of the queen; they drove so close to me that I had to step back to avoid the wheel.

Their Majesties, stepping down, entered the Banqueting Hall by the north door, and having inspected the regalia of Scotland (which had been brought down from the upper room, where it is generally kept), over which four sergeants of Highlanders mounted guard, Their Majesties came out of the further door, and, all alone, the king walked across towards us—I was going to say, the right of the 'line,' but this had, alas! in consequence of the alteration of position, turned into a 'crowd' of veterans. Her Majesty entered the carriage and remained there quietly, while (the staff having by this time arrived) an officer, list in hand, presented us one by one to His Majesty. Unfortunately, the former appeared not to be able to read the list, and I was greeted, when my turn for presentation came, by a peremptory command to me to call out my own name, and almost before I had time to acknowledge the most gracious bow from my king, he was hurried on to the next on the roll; thus His Majesty had no time given to say a word to his old officers.

The king then proceeded down the line, saying a kind word to, and shaking hands with, those of the men he recognised.

Thus, ended what was a very successful parade (in spite of the confusion at the last moment owing to its change on the ground), and a stirring experience—one not likely to be forgotten—a unique roll-call.

Appendix

LIST OF CRIMEAN AND INDIAN MUTINY VETERANS PRESENT ON THE OCCASION OF HIS MAJESTY'S STATE VISIT TO EDINBURGH, MAY, 1903.

General Burroughs, C.B., 93rd Regiment.
General Sprott, Staff, 91st Regiment.
Major-General D. Briggs, Bengal Staff.
Colonel J. P. Robertson, C.B., 31st Regiment.
Colonel Hare, 61st Regiment.
Colonel D. R. Williamson, Coldstream Guards.
Colonel J. H. Middleton, 93rd Regiment.
Captain G. Grant, 93rd Regiment.
Captain Seton, 82nd Regiment.
Captain W. Blackwood, 71st Regiment.
*Captain Burgoyne, 93rd Regiment.
Army Chaplain Rev. Dr. Campbell, Chaplain's Department.
Army Chaplain Rev. H. Dreunan, Chaplain's Department.
*Major P. Chalmers, Scots Fusilier Guards.
*Captain Watt, 92nd Regiment.
Lieutenant Sprott, Royal Scots Greys.

Royal Navy and Naval Reserve.

A.S. A. M'Donald, *Fury.*
A.S. A. Anderson, *Leopard.*
Chief Officer C. Bottrill, *Trafalgar.*
A.S. A. Hepburn, *Rodney.*
Chief Officer G. Williams, Coastguard.
Colour-Sergt. S. Condon, R.M.A.
Pte. T. Wright, R.M.L.I.
A.S. G. Campbell, Naval Reserve.

Royal Horse Artillery.

Gunner H. Falconer.
    ,, P. Chalmers.

4th Dragoon Guards.

Farrier-Major J. Whiteman.
Pte. E. Ferris.

6th Dragoon Guards.

Sergt. E. Lane.

1st Dragoons.

Pte. J. Corbett.
  ,, J. Clark.

Royal Scots Greys.

Q.M.S. J. Masterson.
Sergt. J. Sinclair.
  ,, R. Hunter.
Corpl. P. Ritchie.
Pte. J. Crawford.
  ,, J. Christie.
  ,, J. Drysdale.
  ,, A. Gray.
  ,, J. Hamilton.
  ,, W. Hamilton.
  ,, W. Hammond.
  ,, W. Jackson.

* Unavoidably absent.

196

6th Inniskillings.

Pte. J. Little.

8th R.I. Hussars.

Pte. W. G. J. Fulton.
  „ W. Hunter.

9th Lancers.

Sergt. Chester.

13th Light Dragoons.

Pte. G. Gibson.

16th Lancers.

Pte. J. B. Gentle.

Royal Artillery.

Brig.-Sergt.-Major R. Bell.
Batt.-Sergt.-Major D. M'Donald.
  „ „ „ R. M'Donald.
  „ „ „ R. White.
Sergt. J. Davidson.
  „ W. Goodall.
  „ R. Hammond.
Bombardier W. Taylor.
S.S. T. Larmour.
Gunner Allan.
  „ A. Brodie.
  „ J. Burrell.
  „ G. P. Chissell.
  „ G. Gunn.
  „ J. Hendry.
  „ J. Milne.
  „ J. Ramsden.
  „ T. Smith.
  „ G. Tear.
  „ E. Bolton.
  „ J. Gray.
  „ R. Paisley.
  „ J. Russell.
  „ J. Peters.
  „ W. Bullert.
  „ G. Rae.
  „ J. Conway.

Royal Engineers.

Pte. J. Impet.
  „ W. Lang.
  „ G. Beaton.

Land Transport.

Sergt. A. Hodge.
Pte. J. Grierson.
  „ D. Hunter.
  „ J. Simpson.
  „ J. Anderson.

Grenadier Guards.

Pte. D. Gordon.

Scots Fusilier Guards.

Sergt. P. Adams.
  „ Machray.
  „ D. M'Beth.
Pte. J. Clark.
  „ D. Falconer.
  „ A. M'Farlane.
  „ W. Smith.
  „ W. Wood.
  „ J. Martin.
  „ D. Thomson.
  „ J. Wylie.
  „ J. Rugg.

Royal Scots.

Sergt. R. Robinson.
Pte. P. M'Donald.
  „ T. Price.
  „ J. Sullivan.
  „ W. Cassidy.
  „ J. Molloy.
  „ R. Green.
  „ J. Lundie.
  „ J. Morley.
  „ D. Robertson.
  „ P. Nagle.
  „ W. Stephen.
  „ P. Rooney.
  „ T. Agnew.

4th Foot.

Pte. A. Martin.
  „ J. Harding.

9th Foot.

Pte. W. M'Gill.

14th Foot.

Sergt. G. Mure.

15th Foot.

Colour.-Sergt. J. Austin.

15th Foot.

Pte. A. Christie.

20th Foot.

Pte. J. Cannavan.

21st Scots Fusiliers.

Sergt. J. Clark.
Pte. J. Black.
 „   J. Goffrey.
 „   J. Reynolds.
 „   T. Maide.
 „   M. Finn.

25th Foot.

Pte. G. Mure.

28th Foot.

Pte. T. Anthony.

30th Foot.

Pte. T. Dunlop.
 „   A. Finlay.

33rd Foot.

Pte. Ketterick.

34th Foot.

Pte. W. Boyce.

37th Foot.

Colour-Sergt. J. Rodgers.

39th Foot.

Pte. J. Traynor.

40th Foot.

Corpl. D. M'Leod.

41st Foot.

Sergt. W. Humphries.
Pte. W. Cook.
 „   J. Kelly.
 „   P. Dunn.
 „   P. Haggan.

42nd Foot.

Sergt.-Major J. Steven.
Sergt. J. Dickson.
 „   J. Lillie.
Corpl. A. M'Robbie.

Pte. J. Bryson.
 „   W. Cruickshanks.
 „   R. Downie.
 „   A. Drummond.
 „   R. Fenwick.
 „   A. Hassach.
 „   D. M'Culloch.
 „   J. M'Kenzie.
 „   H. M'Lachlan.
 „   A. Mill.
 „   E. Paterson.
 „   J. Sharkey.
 „   J. Weir.
 „   J. Watt.
 „   J. Gibb.
 „   G. Knowles.
 „   W. Dick.
 „   W. Stewart.
 „   A. Thomson.
 „   T. Mowat.
 „   R. Swan.
 „   G. M'Kay.
 „   J. Logan.
 „   R. S. R. Burns.
 „   W. Brown.
 „   J. Nicholl.
 „   H. Morrison.

46th Foot.

Pte. G. Nairne.

47th Foot.

Pte. F. Rae.

48th Foot.

Pte. A. M'Kenzie.

49th Foot.

Sergt. G. Brown.
Pte. A. Boak.
 „   W. Hefferon.

50th Foot.

Pte. E. Kane.

55th Foot.

Sergt. Steadman.
Pte. T. M'Williams.
 „   J. O'Leary.
 „   J. Stirling.
 „   J. Stanley.

198

60th Rifles and Rifle Brigade.

Sergt. W. Hill.
Pte. J. Barclay.
 „ J. Clark.
 „ J. Robertson.
 „ R. Yarley.
 „ Young.

61st Foot.

Pte. J. Collins.
 „ J. Robertson.

63rd Foot.

Pte. R. M'Nanamara.
 „ J. M'Cabe.

70th Foot.

Pte. R. Robertson.

71st Foot.

Colour.-Sergt. D. Ferguson.
Paymaster-Sergt. W. Phelps.
Sergt. Beveridge.
 „ H. Martin.
 „ W. Nairn.
 „ P. Sinatt.
Pte. W. Black.
 „ J. Brown.
 „ R. Campbell.
 „ J. Danson.
 „ W. Downie.
 „ J. Eadie.
 „ A. Fisken.
 „ J. Gardiner.
 „ J. Gibbons.
 „ A. Hutton.
 „ J. Marr.
 „ R. Mills.
 „ A. Mackay.
 „ A. Taylor.
 „ J. Young.
 „ J. Smith.
 „ J. M'Neill.
 „ G. M'Intosh.
 „ W. Oats.
 „ J. Downie.

72nd Foot.

Sergt. J. M'Intosh.
Corpl. J. Caskie.
Pte. R. Cameron.
 „ A. Chisholm.
 „ M. Christie.

Pte. J. Duncan.
 „ P. Ford.
 „ A. Forrest.
 „ J. S. Gardner.
 „ G. Gyde.
 „ J. Murray.
 „ W. Pullar.
 „ J. Stewart.
 „ J. Stewart.
 „ J. Wellings.
 „ J. Demlay.
 „ A. M'Kenzie.
 „ W. Burton.
 „ J. M'Guire.
 „ J. Grant.
 „ W. Ramsay.
 „ D. Sutherland.
 „ A. Laing.

74th Foot.

Pte. J. Fairfoul.
 „ R. M'Alister.

77th Foot.

Pte. D. M'Kenzie.
 „ Thomson.

78th Foot.

Sergt.-Major J. Pocock.
Bandmaster J. A. Bunce.
Colour-Sergt. R. Brownlee.
Lance-Sergt. Laurie.
Pte. D. Ramage.
 „ D. Russell.
 „ J. B. Thomson.
 „ J. Foley.

79th Foot.

Sergt.-Major S. Currie.
Q.M.S. J. Knight.
 „ J. M'Kenzie.
Colour-Sergt. S. Wells.
 „ J. M'Pherson.
Sergt. R. Henderson.
 „ R. Irvine.
 „ H. M'Kay.
Lance-Sergt. J. Anderson.
Corpl. R. Martin.
Piper J. Hendrie.
Pte. J. Arthur.
 „ J. Brown.
 „ P. Cameron.
 „ W. Gilchrist.

Pte. P. Gray.
„ T. Hunter.
„ T. Hastie.
„ J. Irvine.
„ A. Kerr.
„ J. Melville.
„ T. M'Donald.
„ J. M'Pherson.
„ D. Reid.
„ M. Stewart.
„ W. T. Telfer.
„ R. Thomson.
„ W. Stewart.
„ R. Verner.
„ J. Clelland.
„ J. Stark.
„ J. B. Kidd.
„ J. Murray.
„ W. Hogg.
„ R. Robertson.

80th Foot.

Pte. M. M'Pherson.
„ M. Carmichael.

89th Foot.

Pte. D. Copeland.

90th Foot.

Pte. J. Gibney.
„ D. Greig.
„ A. Livingston.
„ J. M'Garry.

91st Foot.

Pte. J. M'Peake.

92nd Foot.

Colour-Sergt. J. Gilmour.
Drum-Major T. Walker.
Corpl. W. Stoddart.
„ T. Drawbell.
Pte. W. Cruickshank.
„ D. M'Ewen.
„ A. Ross.
„ J. Rankine.
„ Strathdee.
„ R. King.
„ J. Brownlee.
„ J. Crawford.

93rd Foot.

Sergt.-Major J. Motion.
Drum-Major J. Rattray.
Colour-Sergt. J. Hutton.
Sergt. D. M'Broom.
„ A. Christie.
„ W. Fulton.
„ F. Murphy.
„ G. Martin.
„ J. Cook.
„ J. Bryce.
„ J. Cobb.
„ T. Collins.
„ J. Crighton.
„ J. Dickson.
„ H. Douglas.
„ R. Douglas.
„ E. Sage.
„ R. Whittaker.
Corpl. W. Falkner.
„ W. M'Kay.
„ Wright.
Bandsman W. Webster.
Pte. T. Abbot.
„ Baird.
„ R. Brash.
„ A. Ferguson.
„ W. Fraser.
„ J. Gillespie.
„ W. Gillespie.
„ R. Green.
„ J. D. Maxwell.
„ J. Morris.
„ H. Morrison.
„ R. Munro.
„ D. M'Donald.
„ J. M'Donald.
„ D. M'Intosh.
„ J. M'Intosh.
„ D. M'Kenzie.
„ M'Kenzie.
„ J. M'Dougall.
„ A. Rough.
„ W. Russell.
„ J. Stirling.
„ J. Shepherd.
„ J. Taylor.
„ J. Watson.
„ R. Cunningham.
„ J. Duff.
„ J. Morrison.
„ J. Moncreiffe.
„ A. Minto.

Pte. S. Gunn.
 ,, R. Brand.
 ,, Gray.
 ,, D. Cameron.
 ,, A. Keddie.
 ,, A. Cameron.
 ,, H. Anderson.
 ,, J. Hutton.
 ,, G. Campbell.

95th Foot.

Pte. J. Flynn.
 ,, S. Beverley.

97th Foot.

Pte. B. Wolfe.

104th Foot.

Colour-Sergt. P. M'Guire.

3rd Bengal.

Pte. B. Munn.
 ,, W. Wright.

Bengal Artillery.

Pte. J. Smith.

Madras Artillery.

Pte. J. Cossar.

LEONAUR

ALSO FROM LEONAUR
AVAILABLE IN SOFTCOVER OR HARDCOVER WITH DUST JACKET

ZULU:1879 *by D.C.F. Moodie & the Leonaur Editors*—The Anglo-Zulu War of 1879 from contemporary sources: First Hand Accounts, Interviews, Dispatches, Official Documents & Newspaper Reports.

THE RED DRAGOON *by W.J. Adams*—With the 7th Dragoon Guards in the Cape of Good Hope against the Boers & the Kaffir tribes during the 'war of the axe' 1843-48'.

THE RECOLLECTIONS OF SKINNER OF SKINNER'S HORSE *by James Skinner*—James Skinner and his 'Yellow Boys' Irregular cavalry in the wars of India between the British, Mahratta, Rajput, Mogul, Sikh & Pindarree Forces.

A CAVALRY OFFICER DURING THE SEPOY REVOLT *by A. R. D. Mackenzie*—Experiences with the 3rd Bengal Light Cavalry, the Guides and Sikh Irregular Cavalry from the outbreak to Delhi and Lucknow.

A NORFOLK SOLDIER IN THE FIRST SIKH WAR *by J W Baldwin*—Experiences of a private of H.M. 9th Regiment of Foot in the battles for the Punjab, India 1845-6.

TOMMY ATKINS' WAR STORIES: 14 FIRST HAND ACCOUNTS—Fourteen first hand accounts from the ranks of the British Army during Queen Victoria's Empire.

THE WATERLOO LETTERS *by H. T. Siborne*—Accounts of the Battle by British Officers for its Foremost Historian.

NEY: GENERAL OF CAVALRY VOLUME 1—1769-1799 *by Antoine Bulos*—The Early Career of a Marshal of the First Empire.

NEY: MARSHAL OF FRANCE VOLUME 2—1799-1805 *by Antoine Bulos*—The Early Career of a Marshal of the First Empire.

AIDE-DE-CAMP TO NAPOLEON *by Philippe-Paul de Ségur*—For anyone interested in the Napoleonic Wars this book, written by one who was intimate with the strategies and machinations of the Emperor, will be essential reading.

TWILIGHT OF EMPIRE *by Sir Thomas Ussher & Sir George Cockburn*—Two accounts of Napoleon's Journeys in Exile to Elba and St. Helena: Narrative of Events by Sir Thomas Ussher & Napoleon's Last Voyage: Extract of a diary by Sir George Cockburn.

PRIVATE WHEELER *by William Wheeler*—The letters of a soldier of the 51st Light Infantry during the Peninsular War & at Waterloo.